Gooseberry Patch

Christmas COOKIES

A collection of incredibly edible cookies, plus nifty packaging & cookie swap how-to's!

D0904420

Gooseberry Patch

An imprint of Globe Pequot
246 Goose Lane
Guilford, CT 06437

www.gooseberrypatch.com

1•800•854•6673

Copyright 2019, Gooseberry Patch 978-1-62093-332-9

Photo Edition is a major revision of *Christmas Cookies.*

All rights reserved. No part of this book may be reproduced or
utilized in any form or by any means, electronic or mechanical,
including photocopying and recording, or by any information
storage and retrieval system, without permission
in writing from the publisher. Printed in Korea.

Do you have a tried & true recipe...

tip, craft or memory that you'd like to see featured in
a **Gooseberry Patch** cookbook? Visit our website at
www.gooseberrypatch.com and follow the
easy steps to submit your favorite family recipe.
Or send them to us at:

Gooseberry Patch
PO Box 812
Columbus, OH 43216-0812

Don't forget to include the number of servings your recipe
makes, plus your name, address, phone number and
email address. If we select your recipe, your name will
appear right along with it...
and you'll receive a **FREE** copy of the book!

Table of

CONTENTS

Come to a COOKIE EXCHANGE

What's a cookie exchange?

It's a simple, quick & easy way for friends & family to swap sweet treats. Arrive with a few dozen of your favorite goodies and leave with a candy-box assortment!

And the treats don't have to be home-baked. Try exchanging layered mixes, candy, chocolate-dipped pretzels, popcorn balls, savory snack mixes or mulled cider and cocoa mixes.

With just a few simple party basics, you'll be ready to hold a cookie swap of your own...it's so easy!

Dedication:

For the kid in all of us...who can't stop at just one cookie!

Appreciation:

Thank you, friends, for sharing your cherished cookie recipes...every one's a keeper!

PLANNING...
Deck the halls, walls & mantels!

Make a special CD music mix of all-time favorites, or you can set your CD player to shuffle for a variety of very merry music.

COOKIE TIME!

Find a roomy table for everyone to place their cookies on when they arrive. Be sure to move chairs away from the table so everyone can easily collect their goodies.

Make tags (we've given you lots of clever ideas!) for all the goodies that will be arriving. Then, everyone will know what treat they're collecting (or sampling)!

Jot down a shopping list of anything you'll want for the party...spiced cider, eggnog, cocoa or punch. Would you like to have a few appetizers for friends to enjoy while chatting?

Here's a handy
CHECKLIST to help...
JUST MARK 'EM OFF AS YOU GO ALONG!

1 Choose a date & time for your get-together.

2 Mail invitations to 6 or 8 friends (so everyone gets a nice assortment of goodies)! Recipe cards make charming invitations or use pretty ribbon to tie a note to a tin cookie cutter. For invites in a jiffy, just copy, cut & color the ones we've provided!

3 Let friends know how many dozen cookies to bring. It's easy...one dozen for each person coming to the swap.

4 Bake your goodies!

Now...ready, set, relax! It's all about having fun and making memories with family & friends.

Frost-Kissed
CUT-OUTS

Nana's Old-Fashioned Sugar Cookies

Ginnie Wible
McMurray, PA

I sprinkle these with fine, colored sugars...there's no need for frosting with their wonderful flavor!

1 c. butter, softened
1 c. sugar
2 eggs, beaten
2 t. vanilla extract
1 c. sour cream
5 c. all-purpose flour

2 t. baking powder
1 t. baking soda
1-1/4 t. salt
1 T. nutmeg
Garnish: fine, colored sugars

Blend butter and sugar until fluffy; set aside. Stir together eggs, vanilla and sour cream; mix well and set aside. Combine flour, baking powder, baking soda, salt and nutmeg. Add flour mixture alternately with egg mixture to the butter mixture; blend well. Chill in refrigerator overnight. Roll out dough, a softball-size amount at a time, on a floured surface with a floured rolling pin. Roll out to 1/16 to 1/8-inch thickness; cut with cookie cutters. Arrange on ungreased baking sheets; sprinkle as desired with colored sugars. Bake at 375 degrees for 5 to 7 minutes, until golden. Cool on a wire rack; store loosely covered. Makes 7 to 8 dozen.

Think what a better world it would be if we all, the whole world, had cookies and milk about three o'clock every afternoon and then lay down on our blankets for a nap.

-Robert Fulghum

Dusen Confectos

Ellie Grisham
Whitewater, WI

These cookies are nice to make with a friend, sister, mom or even the kids...one person can spread jam while the other rolls them in sugar.

2 c. butter, softened
1 c. sugar
1 t. vanilla extract
3-1/4 c. all-purpose flour

1/4 t. salt
1/2 lb. almonds, ground
12-oz. jar raspberry jam
Garnish: sugar

Blend together butter and sugar. Add vanilla; stir well. Stir in flour, salt and almonds. Roll dough out 1/8-inch thick and cut into an even number of matching shapes; arrange on ungreased baking sheets. Bake at 350 degrees for 8 minutes. Spread half the cookies with a thin layer of raspberry jam, reserving the rest for another recipe; top with remaining cookies. Roll in sugar. Let cool on rack. Makes 4 to 5 dozen.

Retro lunchboxes can be found in such terrific colors and patterns, and they make fun gift boxes for sharing cookies!

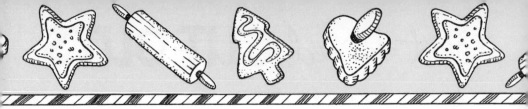

Butterscotch Gingerbread

Kathy Eichhorn
Richmond Hill, GA

This is my mother's recipe and it's my favorite holiday cookie in both fall and winter...the kids love it too!

1/2 c. butter, softened
1/2 c. brown sugar, packed
3.4-oz. pkg. cook & serve
    butterscotch pudding mix
1 egg, beaten
1-1/2 c. all-purpose flour

1/2 t. baking soda
1-1/2 t. ground ginger
1 t. cinnamon
Optional: frosting,
    colored sugars

Blend together butter, brown sugar and pudding; mix well. Beat in egg; stir in remaining ingredients. Chill until slightly firm; roll out dough to 1/4 to 1/2-inch thickness and cut into shapes. Arrange on a greased baking sheet and bake at 350 degrees for 10 to 12 minutes. Decorate as desired. Makes one to 2 dozen.

Mock Whipped Cream Frosting

Brenda Doak
Delaware, OH

Add your favorite food coloring if you like.

1 c. milk
2 T. all-purpose flour
1 c. sugar

1 c. butter
1 t. vanilla extract

Combine milk and flour in a saucepan; cook over medium heat until thickened. Chill. Blend sugar, butter and vanilla in a bowl. Add milk mixture; beat with an electric mixer until whipped. Makes about 3 cups.

Frost-Kissed CUT-OUTS

Cookies for Santa

Leslie Stimel
Clayton, NC

Don't forget these on Christmas Eve!

2/3 c. butter
3/4 c. sugar
1 T. plus 1 t. milk
1 t. vanilla extract

1 egg
2 c. plus 2 T. all-purpose flour
1-1/2 t. baking powder
1/4 t. salt

Blend butter, sugar and milk with an electric mixer on medium speed. Add vanilla and egg; beat well. Add flour, baking powder and salt; mix to combine. Roll out to 1/4-inch thickness and cut with cookie cutters; arrange on ungreased baking sheets and bake at 375 degrees for 7 to 9 minutes. Makes about 2-1/2 dozen.

Send friends & family holiday cards
with a little something extra inside...a cookie cutter
and favorite recipe. What a sweet surprise!

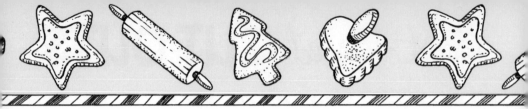

Fancy Puff Cookies

*Lisa McCain
Bartlett, NE*

There's a yummy cream-cheese filling between these sandwich cookies.

2 c. all-purpose flour
1 c. butter, softened
1/2 t. salt
1-1/2 T. half-and-half

1 T. cold water
1 egg white, beaten
Garnish: white and
   colored sugars

Add flour to a large bowl; cut in butter with a fork or pastry cutter until well blended. Combine salt, half-and-half and water; add to flour mixture and stir until liquid is just absorbed. Cover and chill for one hour. Divide into 2 portions; roll out 1/4-inch thick on a floured surface. Cut out with a 1-1/2 inch round cutter; arrange on ungreased baking sheets. Brush with beaten egg white; sprinkle half with white sugar and half with colored sugar. Bake at 350 degrees for 5 to 8 minutes, just until golden. Let cool; spread white sugar cookies with filling and top with colored sugar cookies. Makes 2 to 3 dozen.

Filling:

1 c. powdered sugar
1/2 c. butter, softened

1 T. cream cheese, softened
1 t. vanilla extract

Combine all ingredients; mix until creamy.

Turn Christmas treats into sweetly wrapped treasures...use pretty papers, handcrafted tags and cheery red & white ribbons.

12

Frost-kissed CUT-OUTS

White Velvet Cut-Outs

Dawn Gorenschek
Van Dyne, WI

These are by far the best sugar cookies I've ever had!

2 c. butter, softened
8-oz. pkg. cream cheese,
　softened
2 c. sugar

2 egg yolks, beaten
1 t. vanilla extract
4-1/2 c. all-purpose flour
Optional: candy sprinkles

Blend together butter and cream cheese; add sugar, egg yolks and vanilla. Gradually add flour. Chill for 2 hours; roll out on a floured surface to 1/4-inch thickness. Cut into desired shapes; place on greased baking sheets and bake at 350 degrees for 10 to 12 minutes. Let cool completely and frost; top with sprinkles, if desired.
Makes 7 dozen.

Frosting:

3-1/2 c. powdered sugar,
　divided
3 T. butter
1 T. shortening

1/2 t. vanilla extract
1/4 c. milk
Optional: food coloring

Combine 1-1/2 cups sugar, butter, shortening, vanilla and milk; beat until smooth. Add remaining sugar and food coloring, if desired; beat with an electric mixer on medium speed for 3 minutes until creamy.

Keep your soft cut-outs soft by adding one or 2 apple quarters to the cookie jar...just remove the apples in 2 days.

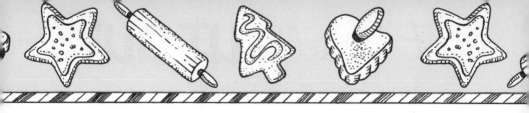

Knapp Kuchen

Rene Gusterson
Oakland, NJ

This was my Great Aunt Marge's recipe. Her cookie cutters and recipes were handed down to me when I got married, and I use them every winter to make these cookies with my daughter, Jenna.

1/2 c. butter, softened
1 c. sugar

5 eggs, beaten
4 c. all-purpose flour

Blend together butter and sugar in a medium bowl; set aside. Combine eggs and flour in a separate bowl; mix well. Add to butter mixture and mix to a dough consistency. Roll out to 1/4-inch thickness and cut with cookie cutters; arrange on greased baking sheets. Bake at 325 degrees for 12 to 15 minutes. Let cool completely and decorate as desired. Makes 5 to 6 dozen.

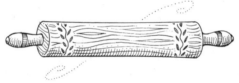

Caramel Icing

Karen Stoner
Delaware, OH

This icing works for topping cake, brownies, cookies...even ice cream!

1 c. buttermilk
1 c. butter, softened
1 t. baking soda

2 c. sugar
1 t. vanilla extract

Mix all ingredients together except vanilla in a saucepan over medium heat. Stir mixture until it reaches the soft-ball stage, or 234 to 243 degrees on a candy thermometer. Remove from heat; add vanilla. Beat until mixture turns a caramel color and is thick enough to spread. Makes about 4 cups.

Crofani

Carol Vickers
New Philadelphia, OH

When my mother came from Italy she brought many warm memories, wonderful stories and treasured traditions. This recipe for pastry was her grandmother's and something she fondly remembered.

2 c. all-purpose flour
2 t. baking powder
3 T. sugar
2 eggs, beaten

3 T. butter, softened
1/2 to 3/4 c. milk
oil for frying
Garnish: powdered sugar

Sift flour, baking powder and sugar together; add eggs and butter a little at a time. Stir in milk a little at a time until mixture is the consistency of pie dough; knead well. Roll out dough to 1/4-inch thickness on a floured surface. Cut into 2"x1" squares or cut with cookie cutters as desired. Heat 1 to 2 inches oil in a skillet over medium-high heat; drop in dough pieces and fry, a few at a time, until puffy and lightly golden. Remove with a slotted spoon; drain on paper towels. Sprinkle with powdered sugar when cool. Store in an airtight container. Makes about 10 dozen.

A recipe for cheer! Cover a cardboard recipe box with colorful paper using spray adhesive. Wrap cookies in tissue paper and tuck inside. Don't forget to jot down the cookie recipe on a recipe card and tie to the box with a pretty ribbon.

Orange-You-Glad Cookies

Jackie Balla
Walbridge, OH

I get requests for this cookie recipe all the time!

1 c. butter, softened
1 c. sugar
1 egg, beaten
2-1/2 c. all-purpose flour

1 t. baking powder
2 T. orange juice
1 T. vanilla extract

Combine butter, sugar and egg in a large mixing bowl; beat with an electric mixer on medium speed until creamy, about one to 2 minutes. Add flour, baking powder, orange juice and vanilla; continue mixing an additional one to 2 minutes. Cover and chill for 2 to 3 hours until dough is firm. Roll dough to 1/4-inch thickness and cut into shapes with cookie cutters. Place one inch apart on lightly greased baking sheets. Bake at 350 degrees for 6 to 10 minutes until edges are lightly golden. Cool and frost. Makes 2 dozen.

Frosting:

3 c. powdered sugar
1/3 c. butter, softened
1 t. vanilla extract

1 to 2 T. orange juice
Optional: red and yellow
    food coloring

Combine all ingredients; beat until fluffy.

Nestle bite-size cookies inside a teacup...what a thoughtful gift.

Spicy Ginger Cookies

Rebecca Chrisman
Citrus Heights, CA

To save time during the holidays, I prepare this cookie dough about 3 months ahead of time and freeze it.

3 c. all-purpose flour
1 t. baking soda
1/4 t. salt
2 t. ground ginger
1 t. cinnamon
1/2 t. nutmeg
1/4 t. ground cloves

3/4 c. shortening
3/4 c. brown sugar, packed
1/2 c. molasses
1 egg, beaten
Garnish: frosting, colored sugar,
    candy sprinkles, raisins

Combine flour, baking soda, salt and spices; set aside. Blend together shortening and brown sugar until light and fluffy; beat in molasses and egg. Stir in flour mixture just until combined. Refrigerate at least 2 hours or overnight. Divide dough into 4 portions; roll out each portion 1/4-inch thick on a floured surface. Flour cookie cutters and cut into desired shapes. Arrange on greased baking sheets; bake at 350 degrees for 10 to 12 minutes. Let cool on wire racks. Frost and decorate as desired. Makes 4 dozen.

Make a frost-kissed snowman! Ice 3 round cut-out cookies with white icing, then arrange on a plate to resemble a snowman. Add colorful candies for a cheery face and buttons, then tie on a licorice whip scarf and add a gumdrop hat. The kids will love him!

Chocolate Cut-Outs

Nancy Cavagnaro
Mountain View, CA

You'll have a hard time eating just one!

1 egg, beaten
2/3 c. butter, softened
3/4 c. sugar
1 t. vanilla extract
1/4 c. baking cocoa

1-1/2 c. all-purpose flour
1 t. baking powder
1/2 t. salt
Optional: frosting, colored sugar

Combine egg, butter and sugar; blend until creamy. Add remaining ingredients. Form dough into 2 flattened rounds; chill. Roll out on a floured surface to 1/8-inch thickness. Cut with cookie cutters as desired; place on ungreased baking sheets. Bake at 350 degrees for 8 to 10 minutes. Let cool; frost and sprinkle with sugar, if desired. Makes 2 to 3 dozen.

Peanut Butter Frosting

Kendall Hale
Lynn, MA

Try this paired with Chocolate Cut-Outs for a delicious taste.

1/2 c. creamy peanut butter
5 T. margarine, softened

1 c. powdered sugar
Optional: 1 to 3 T. milk

Beat peanut butter and margarine with an electric mixer on medium speed. Add sugar; beat to desired consistency. Add milk if too thick. Makes about 2 cups.

No time to frost Chocolate Cut-Outs?
Just top with a stencil and gently dust with
powdered sugar or glittery sanding sugar...beautiful!

Frost-kissed **CUT-OUTS**

Best-Ever Sugar Cookies

*April Gadoury
Coventry, RI*

A soft sugar cookie with a hint of maple flavor!

1-1/4 c. sugar
1 c. butter, softened
2 eggs, beaten
1/4 c. maple-flavored syrup
1 T. vanilla extract
3-1/2 c. all-purpose flour,
   divided

3/4 t. baking powder
1/2 t. baking soda
1/2 t. salt
Optional: candy sprinkles,
   chopped nuts,
   mini semi-sweet
   chocolate chips, frosting

Combine sugar and butter in a large bowl. Beat with an electric mixer on medium speed until well blended. Add eggs, syrup and vanilla; mix well and set aside. Combine 3 cups flour, baking powder, baking soda and salt; beat into sugar mixture gradually on low speed. Mix until well blended; divide into 4 portions. Wrap with plastic wrap and refrigerate for one hour to overnight. Sprinkle one tablespoon remaining flour onto a length of wax paper; place one dough portion on top. Flatten slightly; turn over, add more flour and another length of wax paper. Roll dough to 1/4-inch thickness; cut out with floured cookie cutters. Place 2 inches apart on ungreased baking sheets. Decorate as desired with sprinkles, nuts or chocolate chips, or leave plain to be frosted later. Bake at 375 degrees for 5 to 9 minutes. Makes 3 to 4 dozen.

Whoever heard of a regular home
without a cookie jar?
'twould be a drab situation indeed.
    -Alice M. Child

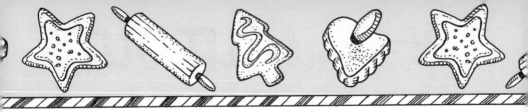

Cocoa-Almond Cut-Outs

Vickie
Gooseberry Patch

Chopped almonds add a nutty crunch to these cut-out cookies.

3/4 c. butter, softened
14-oz. can sweetened
   condensed milk
2 eggs
1 t. vanilla extract
1/2 t. almond extract

2-3/4 c. all-purpose flour
2/3 c. baking cocoa
2 t. baking powder
1/2 t. baking soda
1/2 c. chopped almonds

Combine butter, condensed milk, eggs, vanilla and almond extract in a large mixing bowl; mix well and set aside. Combine flour, cocoa, baking powder and baking soda; gradually add to butter mixture until well blended. Stir in almonds. Divide dough into 4 portions; wrap each in plastic wrap and flatten into a disk. Chill for 2 hours; remove each portion when ready to roll out. Roll out on a floured surface to about 1/8-inch thickness. Cut into desired shapes. Arrange on lightly greased baking sheets and bake at 350 degrees for 6 to 8 minutes. Cool completely on wire racks. Makes 6 dozen.

Keep an eye out at flea markets and tag sales for vintage silver spoons to tie onto jars of homemade cocoa mix.

Herbed Sugar Cookies

Kathy Grashoff
Fort Wayne, IN

Wrap these up and give to your favorite gardening friend.

1 c. butter, softened
1-1/4 c. sugar
1 egg, beaten
2-2/3 c. all-purpose flour

1/2 t. salt
2 T. fresh thyme, chopped
2 T. fresh rosemary, chopped

Beat butter with an electric mixer on medium speed until creamy; gradually add sugar, beating well. Blend in egg; set aside. Combine flour and salt; add to butter mixture, beating at low speed until blended. Stir in herbs. Divide dough into 4 portions; roll each portion to a 1/4-inch thickness on a lightly floured surface. Cut dough with assorted tree-shaped cookie cutters; arrange on ungreased baking sheets. Bake at 350 degrees for 8 to 10 minutes or until lightly golden. Let cool one minute on sheets. Remove to wire racks to cool completely. Makes 3 to 4 dozen.

Layers of sweetness...fill an aluminum canister, available at craft stores, with a stack of round cookies. Twist on the lid, wrap with ribbon, tie on a jingle bell and a tag. A gift in a jiffy!

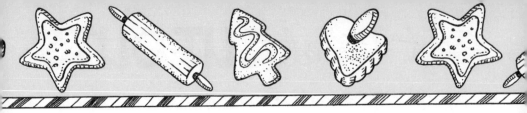

Christmas Sugar Hands

Georell Bracelin
Bend, OR

My brothers and I looked forward to these cookies every year. One by one we would place our hands on the dough while my mother traced around our fingers. Then we would carefully arrange the cookies on tin sheets and watch them bake in the oven. We would frost them ourselves, creating rings, watches and painted fingernails on our very own sugar "hands."

1 c. shortening
1 c. sugar
2 eggs, beaten
1-1/2 t. vanilla extract

2-1/2 c. all-purpose flour
1-1/2 t. baking powder
Optional: 1/2 t. salt
Garnish: frosting

Mix together shortening and sugar; stir in eggs and vanilla. Add dry ingredients; mix well. Chill in refrigerator for at least one hour to overnight. Roll out on a floured surface to 1/4-inch thickness; gently place hands on dough and trace with a butter knife. Arrange on ungreased baking sheets. Bake for 10 minutes at 350 degrees. Let cool on wire racks; frost as desired. Makes 2 to 3 dozen.

Butter versus margarine...butter always gives cookies a richer flavor. Margarine will work for baking, but be sure to avoid low-fat, liquid and soft spreads.

Frost-Kissed CUT-OUTS

Sand Tarts

Shelley Berrier
Belleville, PA

*Knowing how much my dad loves these cookies, I can't let a
Christmas go by without baking him some Sand Tarts!*

1-1/4 c. margarine, softened
2 c. sugar
2 eggs, beaten
4 c. all-purpose flour

powdered sugar
1 to 2 egg whites, beaten
Garnish: colored sugar,
   walnut halves

Blend together margarine and sugar; stir in eggs. Add flour and mix
well. If necessary, add more flour so that dough is not sticky. Roll out
dough as thinly as possible on a surface sprinkled with powdered
sugar. Cut out as desired with cookie cutters. Place on ungreased
baking sheets; brush each cookie with egg white and sprinkle with
colored sugar. Press a walnut half onto each cookie. Bake at
350 degrees for 4 minutes on bottom oven rack; move to top oven
rack and bake an additional 4 minutes. Watch carefully to avoid
burning. Makes 8 to 10 dozen.

*Be original...fill a Chinese take-out box
with homemade cookies for gift-giving!*

23

Icebox Cookies

Barbara Martin
Menominee, MI

When my mother and I made these cookies, she would bake and I would decorate. Many of the cookies were given to family & friends and I felt proud to know someone else got to enjoy my masterpieces!

3/4 c. butter, softened
3/4 c. shortening
1 c. sugar
1 c. brown sugar, packed
3 eggs, beaten
1 t. vanilla extract
2 t. baking soda

1/2 c. water
4 c. all-purpose flour
1 t. salt
1 t. cinnamon
Optional: 3/4 c. finely chopped
   nuts, frosting

Blend together butter, shortening and sugars. Add eggs and vanilla; add nuts if using. Mix well and set aside. Stir baking soda into water; set aside. Mix dry ingredients; stir into butter mixture, alternating with baking soda mixture. Dough will be soft and sticky. Freeze dough for 24 hours. Roll out small amounts of chilled dough on a floured surface 1/4-inch thick; cut with cookie cutters. Arrange on greased baking sheets; bake for 8 to 10 minutes at 350 degrees. Frost as desired. Makes 5 to 6 dozen.

FOR YOU!

Fill each cup of an old-fashioned muffin tin with a different type of cookie...what a tasty sampler!

Holiday Butter Cookies

Debi DeVore
Dover, OH

These will be one of your most-asked-for recipes.
So simple and delicious.

2 c. butter, softened
2 c. powdered sugar
4 eggs, beaten
1 t. baking soda

1 t. lemon juice
1 T. milk
5-1/2 c. all-purpose flour

Blend together butter, powdered sugar and eggs in a large mixing bowl; set aside. Dissolve baking soda in lemon juice; add to butter mixture. Stir in milk and flour gradually. Roll dough to 1/4-inch thickness and cut with cookie cutters. Arrange on ungreased baking sheets; bake at 350 degrees for 8 minutes. Makes 6 to 7 dozen.

Warm cookies dipped in cold
milk...one of life's simple pleasures.

-Unknown

Kolacky

Barbara Ann Rouse
Reseda, CA

Kolacky is a Polish pastry my grandmother made. My job was making the thumbprint, and to be the first one to taste the Kolacky just out of the oven.

1-1/2 c. all-purpose flour
1/2 t. baking powder
1 c. butter, softened
8-oz. pkg. cream cheese,
    softened
1 T. milk

1 T. sugar
1 egg yolk, beaten
12-oz. can fruit or
    poppy seed filling
Garnish: powdered sugar

Combine flour and baking powder in a small bowl; set aside. Blend butter, cream cheese, milk and sugar; add egg yolk, then flour mixture. Form dough into a ball; wrap in wax paper and chill for several hours or overnight. Roll out 1/4-inch thick on a floured surface; cut out with a 2-inch round cookie cutter. Arrange 3 inches apart on ungreased baking sheets. Make a thumbprint impression in center of each round; fill with one teaspoon filling. Bake at 400 degrees for 10 minutes or until golden. Remove to a platter; let cool and sprinkle with powdered sugar. Makes about 4 dozen.

When cookie baking is
a family affair,
dress little ones in
washable clothes and aprons.
Be sure to take lots of pictures!

Lemon Zest Cookies

Weda Mosellie
Phillipsburg, NJ

Pastries are a big part of our Italian family's Christmas tradition,
including these cookies.

3 c. all-purpose flour
4 eggs, beaten
8-oz. pkg. cream cheese,
    softened
1 c. sugar

1/4 c. oil
juice and zest of 2 lemons
1/2 t. baking powder
1/2 t. baking soda

Combine all ingredients in a large mixing bowl; mix well to form a
dough. Roll out to 1/2-inch thickness and chill for one hour. Cut into
circles using a glass or round cookie cutter. Arrange on a greased
baking sheet and bake at 350 degrees for 13 to 15 minutes; let cool.
Dip tops of cookies into glaze; let dry. Makes 2 to 2-1/2 dozen.

Glaze:

1 c. powdered sugar
zest of 1 lemon

juice of 1 to 2 lemons

Combine powdered sugar and zest. Add enough lemon juice to make
a thin consistency, mixing well.

Mmm, instead of
frosting the tops of
cut-out cookies, frost
the bottoms of two
cookies and gently press
together to make a sweetly simple cookie sandwich.

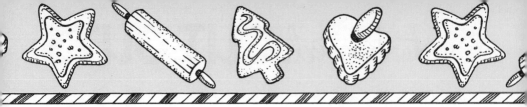

Pepparkakor

Virginia Watson
Scranton, PA

This is a Swedish cookie commonly made for St. Lucia's Day.

1-1/2 c. butter, softened
2-1/4 c. sugar, divided
2 eggs, beaten
1/2 c. molasses
4 c. all-purpose flour

1 T. ground ginger
1-1/2 t. cinnamon
1-1/2 t. ground cloves
2 t. baking soda
1/2 t. salt

Blend together butter and 2 cups sugar in a medium bowl; add eggs and molasses, mixing well. Stir in remaining ingredients to make a stiff dough, adding more flour if necessary. Roll out on a floured surface to 1/8 to 1/4-inch thickness. Cut with cookie cutters and sprinkle with remaining sugar. Arrange on greased baking sheets; bake at 350 degrees for 5 to 6 minutes or until lightly golden. Makes 5 to 6 dozen.

Metal-rimmed key tags make gift tags a snap.
Simply replace the string with a glittery
silver pipe cleaner, tie on and you're done!

Gingerbread Cookies

Peggy Remizowski
New York Mills, NY

This recipe can be used to make gingerbread houses too!

1 c. shortening	1 T. ground ginger
1 c. sugar	1-1/2 t. baking soda
1 egg, beaten	1 t. cinnamon
1 c. molasses	1 t. ground cloves
2 T. white vinegar	1/2 t. salt
5 c. all-purpose flour	

Blend together shortening and sugar; beat in egg, molasses and vinegar. Sift dry ingredients together; blend into shortening mixture. Chill for at least 3 hours. Roll out 1/4-inch thick on a lightly floured surface. Cut into shapes with cookie cutters; arrange on greased baking sheets. Bake at 350 degrees for 8 minutes. Cool slightly on sheets; remove to wire racks and cool completely. Decorate with frosting. Makes 5 dozen.

Frosting:

4-1/2 c. powdered sugar	1 T. lemon juice
6 T. butter, melted	Optional: few drops food
6 T. milk	coloring
2 T. vanilla extract	

Combine all ingredients in a medium bowl. Beat with an electric mixer on low speed until smooth.

Use a prancing reindeer cookie cutter for Gingerbread Cookies... they'll look sweet-as-can-be dancing around the edges of a favorite plate.

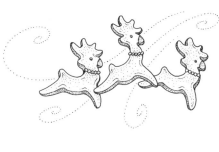

Jean's Sugar Cookies

Glenna Carroll
Golden, OK

This recipe has been in my family for over 40 years. I remember the first time my mother made it when I was 10 years old. Over the years, my children's teachers have requested it for school parties, I've made it for my son's office, and I even sell it in our country store on special occasions. What great memories I have from these wonderful cookies!

1/2 c. shortening	3-1/2 c. all-purpose flour
1/2 c. butter, softened	2 t. baking powder
1 c. sugar	1-1/2 t. vanilla extract
3 eggs, beaten	

Blend together shortening and butter, gradually adding sugar. Add eggs; beat well. Blend in remaining ingredients until smooth. Chill for at least 3 hours or overnight. Divide dough in half. Roll out one half on a lightly floured surface to 1/4-inch thickness, chilling remaining half until ready to use. Cut into shapes with floured cookie cutters; arrange cookies on ungreased baking sheets. Bake at 350 degrees for 10 to 12 minutes until edges are golden. Cool completely on wire racks before frosting. Makes 4 to 5 dozen.

Frosting:

3 T. butter, softened	2-1/2 to 3 T. evaporated milk
2-1/2 to 3 c. powdered sugar	1 t. vanilla extract

Cream butter; beat in sugar alternately with milk and vanilla, adding more sugar or milk as needed to make frosting spreadable.

Buttermilk Sugar Cookies

Meri Hebert
Cheboygan, MI

I make these for every holiday...it's the softest cookie ever, and everyone always wants the recipe.

2 c. sugar
2 c. shortening
4 eggs
1 T. vanilla extract
2 c. buttermilk
6 c. all-purpose flour

1 T. plus 1 t. baking powder
2 t. baking soda
1/2 t. salt
Garnish: 16-oz. container
   favorite frosting
Optional: candy sprinkles

Blend together sugar, shortening and eggs; add vanilla and buttermilk and set aside. Combine flour, baking powder, baking soda and salt; stir into sugar mixture. Add more flour as needed to make a firm dough. Chill for 2 to 3 hours or overnight. Roll out 1/4-inch thick on a floured surface; cut out with cookie cutters. Bake on greased baking sheets at 350 degrees for 7 to 8 minutes. Let cool; frost and decorate as desired. Makes about 6 dozen.

All bundled up! Stitch a square fleece pocket to a warm & fuzzy scarf and tuck plastic-wrapped cut-out cookies into the pocket...a gift that's sure to please.

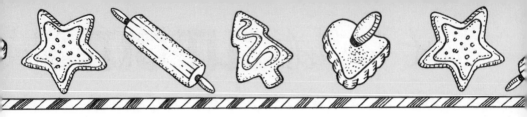

Baby Cakes

Renée Spec
Crescent, PA

These are delicate cookies to make with your smallest cookie cutters. I use a tiny flower-shaped cutter.

1 c. butter, softened
2 c. all-purpose flour

1/3 c. whipping cream
Garnish: sugar

Combine butter, flour and cream; mix well and chill. Roll out 1/8 to 1/4-inch thick on a lightly floured surface. Cut with tiny cookie cutters; place close together on ungreased baking sheets. Pierce each cookie several times with a fork; sprinkle lightly with sugar. Bake at 375 degrees for about 8 minutes, until lightly golden. Assemble cookies in pairs with Creamy Filling. Makes 4-1/2 dozen.

Creamy Filling:

1/4 c. butter, softened
3/4 c. powdered sugar

1 t. vanilla extract

Mix ingredients together until smooth.

Crisp Sugar Cookies

Marie Martin
Vestal, NY

For a fun afternoon, get the kids or friends involved in whipping up this easy cookie recipe...don't forget to take lots of pictures!

2/3 c. butter, softened
3/4 c. sugar
1 t. vanilla extract
1 egg
1 T. plus 1 t. milk
2 c. all-purpose flour

1-1/2 t. baking powder
1/2 t. nutmeg
1/4 t. salt
Garnish: assorted coarse
    decorator sugars

Blend butter, sugar and vanilla. Add egg; beat until light and fluffy. Stir in milk; set aside. Sift together remaining ingredients except garnish and add to butter mixture; mix well. Chill for one hour. Roll out dough 1/8-inch thick on a floured surface; cut with cookie cutters as desired. Place on greased baking sheets; sprinkle with coarse sugar. Bake at 350 degrees for 6 to 8 minutes, until edges are golden. Let cool before removing from baking sheets. Makes 2 dozen.

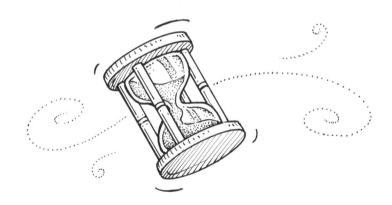

Kids have a hard time waiting for cookie dough to chill. Help pass the time by playing silly games like "I Spy" or "Rock, Paper, Scissors."

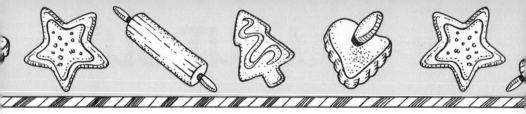

Pepper Cookies

Lisa Ashton
Aston, PA

This spicy little cookie goes great with all the other holiday treats!

1/2 c. butter
1/2 c. sugar
1/2 c. dark corn syrup
1-1/2 t. vinegar
1 egg, beaten
2-1/4 c. all-purpose flour

1/2 t. baking soda
1/2 t. ground ginger
1/2 t. cinnamon
1/2 t. ground cloves
1/4 t. pepper

Melt butter in a medium saucepan; add sugar, corn syrup and vinegar and bring just to a boil. Remove from heat immediately; let cool to room temperature. Stir in egg and set aside. Combine flour, baking soda and spices in a bowl; add to egg mixture, mixing well. Cover and chill for 3 hours to overnight. Divide dough into 4 portions, continuing to chill each portion until ready to roll out. Roll dough onto a lightly floured surface to 1/8-inch thickness. Cut into shapes with cookie cutters and arrange on greased baking sheets. Bake at 375 degrees for 4 to 5 minutes or until golden around the edges. Immediately transfer cookies to cooling rack. Makes 10 dozen.

Use a smaller cookie cutter to create a cut-out inside a cookie. Fill the cut-out with crushed hard candy before baking. As it bakes and melts, the candy magically creates a stained-glass look.

Old-Fashioned Tea Cake Cookies

Wendy Windal
Burkburnett, TX

These will disappear as fast as you can make them!

1 c. shortening
1-1/2 c. sugar
3 eggs
1 t. baking soda
1/2 c. buttermilk
5 c. all-purpose flour
2 t. baking powder
2 t. vanilla extract

Mix shortening, sugar and eggs together; set aside. Dissolve baking soda in buttermilk; stir in flour, baking powder and vanilla. Beat into shortening mixture; roll out on a floured surface to 1/4-inch thickness. Cut with a round cookie cutter; place on ungreased baking sheets. Bake at 400 degrees for 10 to 15 minutes or until golden. Makes 6 to 7 dozen.

Jam Tea

Kristin Blanton
Big Bear City, CA

Try using your favorite flavor of jam...I like this tea with strawberry, apricot or even mint.

4 to 6 t. raspberry jam, divided
1 teapot brewed English
   breakfast tea
sugar to taste
Optional: whipped cream

Place one teaspoon jam in bottom of each teacup; pour hot tea over jam and stir. Add sugar to taste and top with whipped cream, if desired. Makes 4 to 6 cups of tea.

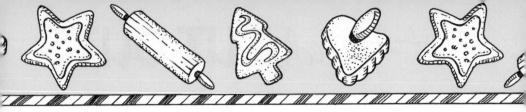

Laurie's Special Sugar Cookies

Laurie Costa
Maxwell, CA

My love of baking came from making delicious cookie creations with my grandma...learning how to measure, how to blend ingredients, and practicing my patience as I waited for the cookies to bake. Now that I have 2 daughters of my own, baking (and eating!) cookies has become our family tradition, especially at Christmas.

2 c. all-purpose flour
1-1/2 t. baking powder
1/4 t. salt
1/4 c. plus 2 T. margarine
1/3 c. shortening

3/4 c. sugar
1 egg, beaten
1 T. milk
1 t. vanilla extract
Optional: cream cheese frosting

Combine flour, baking powder and salt; set aside. Beat margarine and shortening with an electric mixer until soft; add sugar and beat until fluffy. Add egg, milk and vanilla; beat well. Gradually add flour mixture and mix until blended. Cover and chill for 2 hours. Roll dough out 1/8-inch thick on a lightly floured surface. Cut with floured cookie cutters; arrange cookies on greased baking sheets. Bake at 375 degrees for 7 to 8 minutes until just golden around the edges. Cool completely on a wire rack and frost as desired. Makes 1-1/2 to 2 dozen.

For a sweet cookie topping without using frosting, simply dust powdered sugar or baking cocoa over warm cookies.

Old-Fashioned Gingerbread Boys

Christine Waterbury
Sheboygan, WI

*This is my Grandma Rena's recipe. My fondest memories are
of her baking these cookies every Christmas...she always
baked so much love into them.*

1/3 c. shortening	1 t. salt
1 c. brown sugar, packed	1 t. allspice
1-1/2 c. dark molasses	1 t. ground ginger
2/3 c. cold water	1 t. ground cloves
7 c. all-purpose flour	1 t. cinnamon
2 t. baking soda	

Combine shortening, brown sugar and molasses; mix well. Stir in
water; set aside. Sift together flour and remaining ingredients in a
large bowl; add to molasses mixture and mix thoroughly. Divide dough
into 4 portions: chill for 3 to 4 hours. Roll out one portion
at a time, keeping remaining dough cool until ready to use. Roll to
1/2-inch thickness; cut with medium-sized, floured gingerbread boy
cookie cutters. Arrange on greased baking sheets; bake at 375 degrees
for 10 to 12 minutes. Cool completely on wire racks and frost as
desired. Store in airtight containers. Makes about 7 dozen.

Dip cooled cookies halfway into
warm, melted chocolate for a yummy
treat. Set on wax paper to let
chocolate cool and harden.

Christmas Cookies

Flo Burtnett
Gage, OK

Get creative...try making pretty poinsettia leaves on these cookies!

1/2 c. margarine, softened
1/2 c. cream cheese, softened
1-1/4 c. powdered sugar
1 egg
1-1/2 t. vanilla extract

1/4 t. salt
1/4 t. baking powder
3 c. all-purpose flour

Beat margarine, cream cheese and sugar until fluffy; add egg, vanilla, salt and baking powder. Mix in flour until dough holds together; form into a ball. Wrap in plastic wrap; chill for at least one hour. Roll dough out on a floured surface to 1/4-inch thickness; cut with round cookie cutters. Bake at 350 degrees for 15 minutes or until golden; cool. Frost and decorate as desired. Makes 4 to 5 dozen.

Frosting:

2 c. powdered sugar
1/2 t. vanilla extract
2 to 3 T. milk

Garnish: green and red
tube frosting

Combine sugar and vanilla in a small mixing bowl; add enough milk to make a glaze consistency. Mix well; spread on each cookie and let dry. Garnish with red flowers and green leaves on each cookie using tube frosting.

Look for clever containers to tote cookie swap goodies...a vintage milk bottle carrier is ideal.

Frost-Kissed CUT-OUTS

Good Roll-Out Cookies

Debi DeVore
Dover, OH

This recipe makes enough for a cookie swap with plenty left over for friends, neighbors and Santa!

1 T. plus 1 t. baking soda
2 c. sour cream
4 c. butter, softened
4 c. sugar

8 eggs, beaten
2 t. vanilla extract
4 t. baking powder
12 c. all-purpose flour

Dissolve baking soda in sour cream; add butter and sugar. Mix well; stir in eggs and vanilla. Mix in baking powder and flour; roll dough out to 1/4-inch thickness. Cut out with cookie cutters; place on greased and floured baking sheets. Bake at 325 degrees for 8 to 10 minutes; cool. Spread frosting over the top. Makes 12 to 14 dozen.

Frosting:

2-lb. pkg. powdered sugar
2 c. butter, softened
2 to 4 t. vanilla extract

8-oz. pkg. cream cheese, softened
1/4 to 1/2 c. milk

Mix sugar, butter, vanilla and cream cheese together; add enough milk to make desired thickness.

For an extra-special touch, pipe frosting onto cookies in a snowflake, star or tree shape, then dust with sanding sugar...so glittery!

You're invited to a

COOKIE EXCHANGE!

WHEN: _____

HOSTED

BY: _____

WHERE: _____

_____

_____

R.S.V.P. _____

Please bring: _____

Use our invitation to send to family & friends!
Just copy, cut out & color with markers,
colored pencils or glitter pens. oh so easy!

Razzle-Dazzle
DROP COOKIES

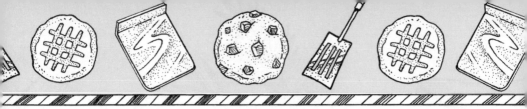

Chewy Molasses Dreams

Lisa Case
Fresno, CA

You'll love eating this spicy, sweet cookie...better than store-bought!

3/4 c. shortening
1-1/2 c. sugar, divided
1 egg
1/3 c. molasses
2-1/3 c. all-purpose flour
2 t. baking soda

2 t. ground ginger
2 t. cinnamon
2 t. nutmeg
1 t. ground cloves
1/4 t. salt

Combine shortening, one cup sugar, egg and molasses; mix well. Blend in flour, baking soda, spices and salt. Shape into one-inch balls; roll in remaining sugar. Arrange on ungreased baking sheets; flatten slightly. Bake at 350 degrees for 7 to 8 minutes. Makes 3 to 4 dozen.

Visit flea markets and gather up vintage colanders,
flour sifters, teapots and teacups...terrific
for tucking cookies into. Don't forget to
tie on a recipe card too!

Razzle-Dazzle DROP COOKIES

Chow Mein Cookies

Mary Freireich
Dublin, OH

Here's a tasty butterscotch cookie with a twist...chow mein noodles!

2 6-oz. pkgs. semi-sweet
   chocolate chips
2 6-oz. pkgs. butterscotch chips
2 3-oz. cans chow mein noodles
1/2 c. cashew pieces

Melt together chocolate and butterscotch chips over low heat in a saucepan; blend well. Stir in chow mein noodles and cashews. Drop by teaspoonfuls onto wax paper-lined baking sheets. Let set until firm. Makes 2 to 3 dozen.

Eggnog

Janet Pritchard
Killeen, TX

It just wouldn't be Christmas without eggnog!

2 c. whipping cream
1/3 c. powdered sugar
1 t. rum extract
1/2 t. nutmeg
1/4 t. allspice
1 qt. vanilla ice cream, softened
4 qts. eggnog, divided
Garnish: cinnamon sticks, if
   desired

Whip cream with powdered sugar, rum extract, nutmeg and allspice until stiff peaks form; set aside. Combine ice cream and 2 cups eggnog in a blender; blend until just smooth. Pour into a large punch bowl; stir in remaining eggnog. Fold in whipped cream mixture just until fluffy. Makes about 5 quarts.

*Cookie cutters make whimsical gift bag tie-ons...
a heart or bunny for springtime, flag for summer,
oak leaf or acorn in the fall and a plump snowman
or snowflake in the winter.*

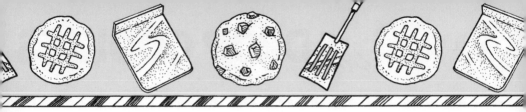

Meringue Kisses

Candy Hannigan
Monument, CO

Try piping these out in different holiday shapes...snowmen are cute with chocolate chips for eyes and buttons, and a cherry for its nose!

3 egg whites
1/4 t. cream of tartar
2/3 c. sugar
1/2 c. mini semi-sweet
   chocolate chips

1/2 t. peppermint extract
several drops red or green
   food coloring

Beat egg whites with an electric mixer on high speed until foamy; beat in cream of tartar. Slowly beat in sugar one tablespoon at a time until dissolved and stiff peaks form. Fold in chocolate chips, extract and food coloring. Drop mixture by teaspoonfuls onto parchment paper-lined baking sheets. Bake at 275 degrees for 30 minutes; turn off oven and leave overnight. Store in an airtight container at room temperature. Makes 2 to 3 dozen.

Fold glittery paper into a cone shape and secure the edges with tape. Fill with a variety of cookies... what a great party favor!

Razzle-Dazzle **DROP COOKIES**

Mint Petites

Debbie Pecore
Charlton, MA

If you're a fan of mint-chocolate, try these!

1/4 c. sugar
1 c. margarine, softened
1/4 to 1/2 t. peppermint extract
1/2 t. vanilla extract

2 c. all-purpose flour
Garnish: vanilla or chocolate
frosting, peppermint or
chocolate mint candies

In a large bowl, blend sugar and margarine together until fluffy.
Add extracts; mix well. Stir in flour and blend well. Shape into
one-inch balls; place on ungreased baking sheets and flatten slightly.
Bake at 375 degrees for 12 minutes or until lightly golden. Let cool.
Frost with vanillia frosting and sprinkle with crushed peppermint
candies, or with chocolate frosting and top with chocolate mints cut
into triangles. Makes 2 to 3 dozen.

White Hot Chocolate

Dawn Brown
Vandenberg AFB, CA

This hot chocolate will warm you head-to-toe.

12-oz. bar white chocolate,
   finely chopped
6 c. milk
2 c. heavy cream

1 t. vanilla extract
Garnish: whipped cream,
   cinnamon, milk chocolate
   shavings, candy canes

Place white chocolate in a medium bowl; set aside. Combine milk and
cream in a saucepan; heat over medium heat until bubbles begin to
form around edges, about 4 minutes. Do not boil. Pour over white
chocolate. When chocolate begins to melt, gently stir to combine.
Whisk in vanilla. Top with whipped cream, cinnamon or chocolate
shavings. Add a candy cane too! Serve immediately. Makes 8 cups.

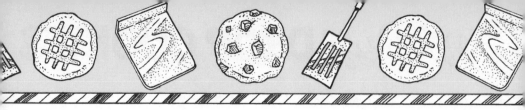

Grandma's Ginger Cookies

Andrea Barclay
Somerset, PA

My Grandma Kintigh used to make these all the time and I ate them with butter on top. I make them now for my friends & family and my kids love them, although they don't use the butter...they just want to eat them!

3/4 c. shortening
1 c. dark brown sugar, packed
1/2 c. dark molasses
1 egg
2 c. all-purpose flour
1/2 t. salt

2 t. baking soda
1 t. cinnamon
1 t. ground ginger
1/8 t. ground cloves
Garnish: sugar

Blend together shortening, sugar, molasses and egg; set aside. Mix together flour, salt, baking soda and spices; add slowly to shortening mixture. Mix well. Place sugar in a small bowl; drop dough by teaspoonfuls into sugar. Roll into balls; arrange on ungreased baking sheets. Bake at 350 degrees for 8 to 10 minutes, until just set and starting to crack. Let stand on baking sheets for one to 2 minutes; remove to cooling racks. Store in an airtight container. Makes 4 to 5 dozen.

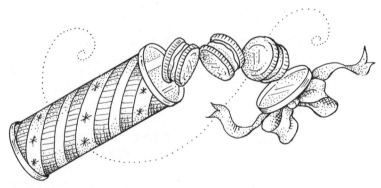

Stack cookies inside an empty oatmeal or potato chip canister that's been covered in pretty paper...just top with a bow!

Holiday Gumdrop Cookies

Pat Habiger
Spearville, KS

Christmas just wouldn't be the same without
Holiday Gumdrop Cookies!

1/2 c. butter, softened	1/2 t. baking soda
1/2 c. margarine, softened	1/4 t. salt
1 c. sugar	2 c. quick-cooking oatmeal,
2 eggs	uncooked
1 t. vanilla extract	1 c. flaked coconut
2 c. all-purpose flour	1 c. pecans, coarsely chopped
1 t. baking powder	1 c. gumdrops, sliced

Blend together butter, margarine and sugar. Stir in eggs, one at a time, and vanilla until well mixed; set aside. Sift together flour, baking powder, baking soda and salt; add to butter mixture and mix well. Stir in remaining ingredients just until mixed; refrigerate dough several hours or overnight. With floured hands, roll dough into 1-1/2 inch balls. Bake on parchment paper-lined baking sheets for 10 to 15 minutes at 375 degrees. Makes 2 to 3 dozen.

Want ready-made cookies at your fingertips? Just freeze them! Most cookie doughs freeze well and will stay fresh for 4 to 6 weeks and baked cookies for 3 to 4 weeks. When it's cookie baking time, just let them come to room temperature and bake according to the recipe.

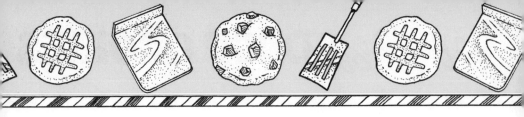

Brown Sugar Drops

Andrea Barclay
Somerset, PA

*My husband's grandmother gave this recipe to me shortly after
we were married. She doesn't bake anymore, so now it's nice
that we can make these cookies for her.*

1 egg, beaten
1 c. brown sugar, packed
1 t. vanilla extract
1/2 c. all-purpose flour

1/4 t. baking soda
1/4 t. salt
1-1/2 c. chopped walnuts

Stir together egg, brown sugar and vanilla. Stir in flour, baking soda
and salt; add walnuts. Drop by teaspoonfuls onto well-greased, floured
baking sheets. Bake at 350 degrees for 7 to 9 minutes or until cookies
start to turn golden at edges. Remove from baking sheets immediately.
Makes about 4 dozen.

Mexican Hot Chocolate

Jen Licon-Conner
Gooseberry Patch

This is serious hot chocolate...almost a dessert in itself!

3.3-oz. tablet Mexican
   chocolate, diced

1-1/4 c. milk
1-1/4 c. half-and-half

Combine all ingredients in a saucepan;
bring to a simmer, stirring until chocolate
is melted and well combined. Stir with a
whisk until fluffy before serving.
Makes 2-1/2 cups.

Pecan Crispies

Emily Robinette
Xenia, OH

Grandma Alice made these every Christmas and topped them with red and green sugar. For me, making them pretty took a little more practice. Don't worry if they don't look perfect...they sure will taste perfect!

1/2 c. shortening
1/2 c. margarine, softened
2-1/2 c. brown sugar, packed
2 eggs, beaten
2-1/2 c. all-purpose flour

1/2 t. baking soda
1/4 t. salt
1 c. chopped pecans
Garnish: sugar

Combine shortening, margarine and brown sugar; mix well. Beat in eggs; set aside. Sift together flour, baking soda and salt; add to shortening mixture and mix well. Stir in pecans. Drop by heaping teaspoonfuls about 3 inches apart onto greased baking sheets. Press down using a greased, sugared glass; sprinkle tops with sugar. Bake at 350 degrees for 12 to 15 minutes; cookies will be dark when done. Makes 3 to 4 dozen.

To minimize spreading in drop cookies, let the baking sheets cool between batches and only grease them if the recipe calls for it.

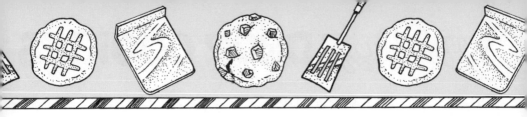

Health Nut Cookies

Cyndi Little
Whitsett, NC

This recipe came from a good friend in our community…she entered it in a baking contest in the 50's and won a brand-new range presented to her by Ronald Reagan! She thought it was so special, she never took the plastic off!

1 c. butter	1-1/2 t. baking powder
1 c. brown sugar, packed	1/2 t. salt
1 c. sugar	1 c. chopped dates
2 eggs	1 c. raisins
1 t. vanilla extract	1 c. flaked coconut
2 c. all-purpose flour	1 c. chopped pecans
1-1/2 c. quick-cooking oats, uncooked	Optional: pecan halves

Blend together butter, sugars, eggs and vanilla; add flour, oats, baking powder and salt. Mix well. Stir in dates, raisins, coconut and pecans. Drop by teaspoonfuls onto greased baking sheets; flatten slightly. Top each cookie with a pecan half, if desired. Bake at 325 degrees for 15 minutes. Remove from baking sheets while still warm. Makes about 6 dozen.

A balanced diet is a cookie in each hand.

-Unknown

Razzle-Dazzle DROP COOKIES

Almond-Pine Nut Cookies

Annette Lacombe
Norwich, CT

The taste of almonds and the crunchiness of pine nuts.

7-oz. pkg. almond paste, diced
1/3 c. sugar
2 egg whites, divided

1/2 t. vanilla extract
3 T. all-purpose flour
1/2 c. pine nuts

Beat together almond paste, sugar and one egg white until smooth. Blend in remaining egg white, then vanilla. Stir until flour until dough forms. Drop by heaping teaspoonfuls, 2 inches apart, onto parchment paper-lined baking sheets. Press 1/2 teaspoon pine nuts onto each cookie. Position oven rack in top third of oven; bake at 325 degrees until edges are golden, about 15 minutes. Let cool on wire rack. Makes about 2 dozen.

For an extra touch, roll chilled dough in colored or cinnamon sugar, chopped nuts or flaked coconut.

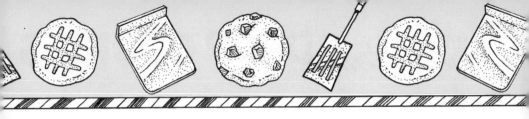

Kris Kringles

Eleanor Bartz
Shelby, IN

The jolly old elf himself can't resist these!

1/2 c. butter, softened	1 t. lemon juice
1/4 c. sugar	1 c. cake flour
1 egg, separated	1/8 t. salt
1 T. orange zest	1/2 c. finely chopped nuts
1 t. lemon zest	9 maraschino cherries, halved

Thoroughly blend butter and sugar. Beat egg yolk; add to butter mixture along with zests and lemon juice. Mix well. Stir in flour and salt. Chill until firm. Form 1/2-inch balls; dip in beaten egg white and roll lightly in nuts. Place on greased baking sheets; press a cherry half in center of each. Bake at 325 degrees for 20 minutes. Makes 1-1/2 dozen.

Parchment paper is terrific for shaping into cones to hold icings for piping. And it's easy to find in rolls, circles or sheets at craft stores or supermarkets with cake-decorating supplies.

Christmas Crinkle Cookies

Rachael Hall
McDonald, PA

Chocolatey morsels with a snowy coating of powdered sugar...yummy!

12-oz. pkg. semi-sweet
   chocolate chips, divided
1-1/2 c. all-purpose flour
1-1/2 t. baking powder
1/4 t. salt

1 c. sugar
6 T. butter, softened
1-1/2 t. vanilla extract
2 eggs
3/4 c. powdered sugar

Place one cup chocolate chips in a microwave-safe bowl. Microwave on high setting for one minute; stir. Microwave at additional 10-second intervals, stirring until smooth. Cool to room temperature. Combine flour, baking powder and salt in a small bowl; set aside. Blend sugar, butter and vanilla in a large bowl; beat in melted chocolate. Add eggs one at a time, stirring well after each. Gradually beat in flour mixture; stir in remaining chips. Chill just until firm. Shape into 1-1/2 inch balls; roll generously in powdered sugar. Place on ungreased baking sheets. Bake at 350 degrees for 10 to 15 minutes, until sides are set and centers are still slightly soft. Cool on baking sheets 2 minutes; place on wire racks to cool completely. Makes 4 to 5 dozen.

Make cookie gifts festive and fun! Stack cookies inside vintage glassware or fill a retro recipe box or old-fashioned ice cream mold. Even the simplest cardboard box or paper bag can be transformed tied up with ribbon and greenery.

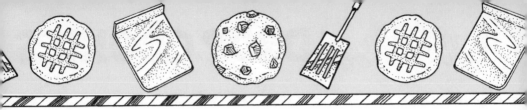

Heavenly Cookies

Joy Diomede
Double Oak, TX

Craving chocolate? Try these double-chocolate and candy bar cookies!

1 c. butter, softened
2-1/2 c. powdered sugar
2 eggs
2 t. vanilla extract
2-1/2 c. all-purpose flour
1 t. baking soda
1 t. salt

1/2 c. white chocolate chips
1-1/2 c. semi-sweet
　 chocolate chunks
4 1.4-oz. toffee candy bars,
　 crushed
Optional: 1/2 c. chopped pecans

Combine butter, sugar, eggs and vanilla; mix well. Add flour, baking soda and salt; mix until well blended. Stir in chocolate chips, chocolate chunks, candy bar pieces and nuts, if using. Drop by tablespoonfuls onto ungreased baking sheets. Bake at 350 degrees for 12 to 15 minutes, or until golden. Makes 2 dozen.

Gooseberry
Patch
Delaware, OH

To: Kris K.
Winter Ln.
North Pole

Shipping cookies is a snap...just follow these pointers. Choose firm cookies such as sliced, drop or bar cookies; avoid frosted or filled ones. Line a sturdy box with plastic bubble wrap and pack cookies in a single layer with wax paper between the layers.

Chocolate Snowballs

Arlene Grimm
Decatur, AL

Rolling cooled cookies in powdered sugar makes these buttery cookies even richer.

2 c. sugar
1/2 c. milk
3/4 c. margarine
6 T. baking cocoa
3 c. quick-cooking oats,
    uncooked

1 c. chopped pecans
1 t. vanilla extract
Garnish: powdered sugar

Combine sugar, milk, margarine and cocoa in a saucepan. Bring to a boil over medium heat, stirring constantly. When mixture comes to a boil, remove from heat; stir in oats, pecans and vanilla. Allow to cool to room temperature. Shape into one-inch balls; roll in powdered sugar. Keep refrigerated in an airtight container. Makes about 3 dozen.

For a whimsical gift, line a vintage pail with a kitchen towel and tuck freshly baked cookies inside.

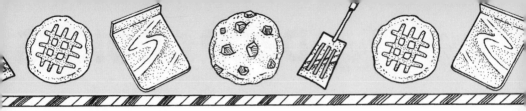

Whoopie Pies

Brenda Doak
Delaware, OH

Not pies at all, but soft, chocolatey cookies!

2 c. sugar
1/2 c. shortening
2 eggs
1 t. vanilla extract
4 c. all-purpose flour
1/2 c. baking cocoa

2 t. baking soda
1/2 t. salt
1 c. milk
1 T. vinegar
1 c. warm water

Blend together sugar, shortening, eggs and vanilla; set aside. Sift together flour, cocoa, baking soda and salt; set aside. Combine milk and vinegar; stir to blend and set aside. Add flour mixture to sugar mixture alternately with milk mixture and warm water. Drop by heaping teaspoonfuls onto lightly greased baking sheets. Bake at 425 degrees for 7 to 10 minutes; let cool. Spread filling on the bottom of one cookie; top with another cookie to make a sandwich. Makes 3 dozen.

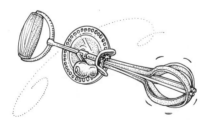

Filling:

1-1/2 c. milk
1/2 c. plus 1-1/2 t. all-purpose
    flour
1/2 c. butter, softened

3/4 c. shortening
1 t. salt
1 t. vanilla extract
2 c. powdered sugar

Combine milk and flour in a saucepan; heat and stir until thick. Refrigerate until chilled. In a mixing bowl, combine chilled milk mixture and remaining ingredients. Beat until fluffy.

Razzle-Dazzle DROP COOKIES

Snow Drops

Kari Mott
Galloway, OH

These are so good with a glass of milk!

1/2 c. margarine, softened
1 c. brown sugar, packed
1 egg
1 T. water
1 t. vanilla extract
1-1/2 c. all-purpose flour

1/2 t. baking soda
1/2 t. cinnamon
1 c. dates, finely chopped
1/2 c. pecans, finely chopped
Garnish: powdered sugar

Blend together margarine, brown sugar, egg, water and vanilla; set aside. Combine flour, baking soda and cinnamon; stir into margarine mixture. Mix in dates and pecans. Drop by tablespoonfuls onto greased baking sheets. Bake for 8 to 10 minutes at 375 degrees. Roll in powdered sugar while still warm. Makes 3 dozen.

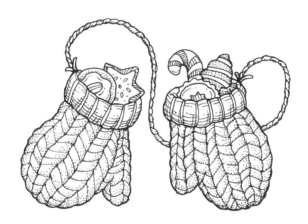

Let the season choose cookie packaging...cookies can be wrapped and tucked inside gardening gloves in summer or woolly mittens in winter. Add a homemade cocoa mix or fruity lemonade mix too!

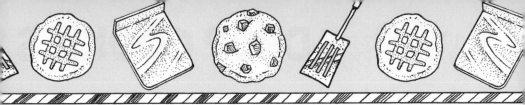

Grandma's Red-Hot Cookies

Susie Pechtl
Fargo, ND

When I was a child and went over to Grandma's house, I would always find these cookies in her kitchen cupboard.

1 c. sugar
1 c. powdered sugar
1 c. butter, softened
1 c. shortening
2 eggs
1/8 t. vanilla extract

4 c. all-purpose flour
2 t. cream of tartar
1 t. baking soda
Garnish: powdered sugar,
    red cinnamon candies

Combine all ingredients except garnish; mix well. Form into a roll; wrap in plastic wrap and chill thoroughly. Roll into one-inch balls; dip in powdered sugar. Flatten slightly with the bottom of a cup; top each with a cinnamon candy. Place on ungreased baking sheets. Bake at 350 degrees for about 9 minutes, watching carefully to avoid burning. Makes 6 dozen.

For a scrumptious change, substitute butterscotch, mint, cherry or cinnamon chips in place of the usual chocolate chips in favorite cookie recipes.

Mom's Cream Cheese-Jelly Cookies

Dawn Menard
Seekonk, MA

A favorite my mother only made at Christmas time.

1 c. butter, softened
2 3-oz. pkgs. cream cheese,
  softened

2 c. all-purpose flour
Garnish: grape jelly

Blend together butter, cream cheese and flour in a large bowl to form dough. Refrigerate for one hour. Shape into one-inch balls; place on ungreased baking sheets. With your thumb, make an indentation on each ball. Bake at 325 degrees for 10 minutes, until golden. Let cool completely; place a spoonful of jelly in each indentation. Makes 2 to 3 dozen.

Holiday Pineapple Punch

Marci Grubb
Columbus, OH

For a festive touch, add a sprig of mint to your ice cube trays before freezing.

2 1-1/2 oz. pkgs. strawberry-
  flavored drink mix
2 c. sugar
4 qts. plus 3/4 c. water, divided
6-oz. can frozen pineapple
  juice concentrate

2-liter bottle lemon-lime soda
2-liter bottle strawberry soda
2-1/2 to 3 c. pineapple sherbet,
  softened

Combine drink mix, sugar and 4 quarts water in a large punch bowl; stir to dissolve. Add juice concentrate and remaining water, mix until concentrate is melted. Add sodas and sherbet; serve over ice. Makes about 2 gallons.

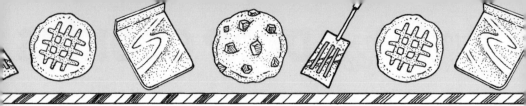

Peanut Butter Criss-Crosses

Jennifer Wiseman
Jamaica Plain, NY

Who doesn't love these traditional favorites? No cookie swap would be complete without them.

1 c. shortening
1 c. sugar
1 c. brown sugar, packed
2 eggs
1 t. vanilla extract

1 c. creamy peanut butter
3 c. all-purpose flour
1 t. baking soda
1 t. salt

Blend together shortening and sugars; mix in eggs and vanilla. Add peanut butter, mixing well. Set aside. Combine flour, baking soda and salt; slowly add to shortening mixture to make a stiff dough. Roll into one-inch balls; place on ungreased baking sheets. Flatten with a floured fork in a criss-cross pattern. Bake at 350 degrees for 9 to 11 minutes, until edges are golden. Makes 5 dozen.

Tie a pretty vintage silver fork on a jar filled with Peanut Butter Criss-Crosses. Just slip the recipe between the fork tines and friends will think of you each time they pull out the recipe!

Potato Chippers

Betty Kiphart
Muncie, IN

This recipe was given to me by a dear friend years ago. They've always been a favorite of mine (and everyone who samples them)!

1 c. shortening
1 c. sugar
1 c. brown sugar, packed
2 eggs
2 c. all-purpose flour

1 t. baking soda
1 t. salt
2 c. potato chips, crushed
1 c. chopped nuts

Blend shortening with sugars; add eggs and mix well. Sift together flour, baking soda and salt; add to shortening mixture. Stir in chips and nuts; shape into one-inch balls. Place on ungreased baking sheets; press down with a floured fork. Bake at 350 degrees for 10 to 12 minutes. Makes about 3 dozen.

A tier of cake plates is a fun way to serve cookies, candy or brownies on a buffet table.

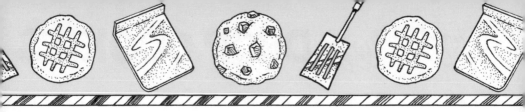

Moravian Spice Crisps

Mary Murray
Mount Vernon, OH

Similar versions of this spice cookie have been around since the 1700's. A crispy favorite...nice with a mug of warm cider.

3/4 c. all-purpose flour
1/2 t. baking powder
1/4 t. baking soda
1/4 t. salt
1/2 t. cinnamon
1/2 t. ground ginger

1/2 t. white pepper
1/4 t. ground cloves
1/3 c. light brown sugar, packed
3 T. butter, softened
1/4 c. light molasses

Combine flour, baking powder, baking soda, salt and spices; set aside. In a mixing bowl, blend brown sugar and butter with an electric mixer at low speed. Beat about 2 minutes on high speed until creamy. Beat in molasses at medium speed until blended. Using a spoon, stir in the flour mixture. Drop by rounded teaspoonfuls about 4 inches apart on greased baking sheets. Press each into a 2-inch circle. Bake at 350 degrees for 8 to 10 minutes. Let cool several minutes; remove to wire rack to cool completely. Store in tightly covered container. Makes about 3 dozen.

Once cookies are tucked inside a box for gift giving, wrap the box in kraft paper. On the box lid, arrange small ivory buttons in the shape of a star or wreath and glue in place. What a simple but sweet decoration.

One-Bowl Macaroons

Suzette Edwards
Glendale, AZ

If you love coconut, you'll love these too!

2 7-oz. pkgs. flaked coconut
14-oz. can sweetened
   condensed milk

2 t. vanilla extract

Mix ingredients well in a large bowl. Drop by teaspoonfuls one inch apart on well-greased baking sheets. Press down slightly; bake at 350 degrees for 10 to 12 minutes. Immediately remove from baking sheets; let cool on a wire rack. Store loosely covered at room temperature. Makes 4 dozen.

Wassail

Sarah Lopez
Jacksonville, FL

Warm, spiced cider...so delicious!

1 gal. apple cider
2 t. whole cloves
2 t. whole allspice

2 sticks cinnamon
2/3 c. sugar

Combine all ingredients in a saucepan; bring to a boil. Reduce to low heat and simmer for 20 minutes. Strain; pour into a punch bowl to serve. Makes 32 servings.

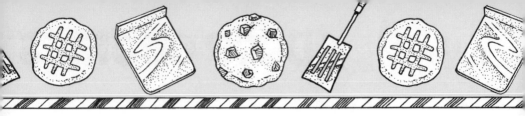

Lebkuchen

Elaine Myers
Fillmore, IN

*Translated, Lebkuchen means "gingerbread," although lots of
versions have no ginger in them at all...like this one. It is, however,
an easy-to-make honey cookie everyone will love!*

4 c. honey
11 c. all-purpose flour, divided
6 eggs
2-1/2 c. sugar
2 T. cinnamon
1 T. ground cloves

1 t. allspice
1 T. ground nutmeg
2 T. lemon juice
1 T. baking soda
Garnish: powdered sugar
　　frosting, whole almonds

Warm honey in a saucepan until thin; place in a very large mixing
bowl. Stir in 6-1/4 cups flour; set aside. Beat eggs until light and thick;
add sugar and beat well. Stir in spices. Mix lemon juice and baking
soda; stir into mixture. Add remaining flour; cover and chill. Drop by
tablespoonfuls onto lightly greased baking sheets. Bake at 350 degrees
for 8 to 10 minutes. When cool, frost cookies and press one almond
onto each. Store in an airtight container. Makes 14 to 16 dozen.

Keep cookies sweet and petite...use mini cookie cutters
or small scoops to make cookies bite-size.
Each one will be a perfect little treat so
friends & family can try one of each variety!

Orange Cookies

DeeAnn Portra
Turtle Lake, ND

My Grandma used to bake these at Christmas. She was a great cook and a very special lady.

1-1/2 c. brown sugar, packed	1-1/2 t. vinegar
3/4 c. butter, softened	3 c. all-purpose flour
2 eggs	1/4 t. salt
1 t. vanilla extract	1-1/2 t. baking powder
1-1/2 t. orange zest	1/2 t. baking soda
1/2 c. milk	Optional: 3/4 c. chopped walnuts

Combine brown sugar, butter, eggs, vanilla and zest, blending after each addition. Set aside. Mix together milk and vinegar; stir to blend and add to brown sugar mixture. Set aside. Combine flour, salt, baking powder and baking soda; blend well and add to brown sugar mixture. Stir in walnuts, if using. Drop by teaspoonfuls onto greased baking sheets. Bake for 8 to 10 minutes at 350 degrees. Frost with Orange Frosting when cool. Makes 3 to 4 dozen.

Orange Frosting:

1/3 c. orange juice	1-1/2 t. orange zest
1 c. powdered sugar	

Combine all ingredients; mix well.

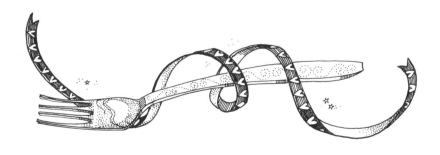

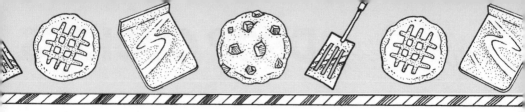

Chocolatey Pumpkin Cookies

Susan Whitney
Fountain Valley, CA

Pumpkin and chocolate go together beautifully!

1 c. shortening
1 c. sugar
1 c. canned pumpkin
1 egg
1 t. vanilla extract
2 c. all-purpose flour

1 t. baking soda
1 t. cinnamon
1/2 t. salt
3/4 c. semi-sweet
    chocolate chips

Blend together shortening, sugar, pumpkin, egg and vanilla; set aside. Sift together flour, baking soda, cinnamon and salt; stir into shortening mixture. Fold in chocolate chips. Drop by tablespoonfuls onto ungreased baking sheet. Bake at 350 degrees for 10 to 12 minutes. Frost cookies when cool. Makes 2 to 3 dozen.

Frosting:

3 T. butter
3 T. milk

1/2 c. brown sugar, packed
1-1/2 to 2 c. powdered sugar

Combine butter, milk and brown sugar in a small saucepan. Boil for 2 minutes; add enough powdered sugar to make a spreading consistency. Mix well.

For a lunchbox surprise, slip cookies inside a vellum envelope and tie closed with shoestring licorice!

Fruit Jewel Cookies

Tammy Thomas
Franklin, PA

Every Christmas is made more special by including these cookies in our baking tradition. My mother has made them every year for the holidays and I always think of her when I bake them.

1/2 c. butter, softened
1/2 c. powdered sugar
1 egg, separated
1/4 c. pineapple preserves
1 t. orange zest
1 t. vanilla extract

1 c. all-purpose flour
1/4 t. salt
1 c. finely chopped pecans
Garnish: candied cherries,
    halved

Blend butter and powdered sugar together until light and fluffy. Stir in egg yolk, preserves, zest and vanilla. Add flour and salt; mix well. Chill for 2 hours. Roll into one-inch balls; dip in beaten egg white, then into chopped pecans. Place on ungreased baking sheets; bake at 350 degrees for 10 minutes. Remove from oven; lightly press a candied cherry half into the top of each cookie. Makes 1-1/2 dozen.

At dessert time, serve several cookies inside colorful vintage dessert cups...little elves are sure to love 'em!

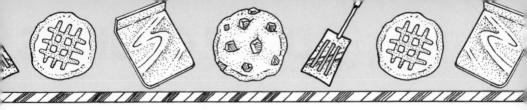

Caramel Apple Cookies

Nichole Martelli
Alvin, TX

You'll be in heaven with just one bite of these rich cookies.

1/2 c. shortening
1-1/4 c. light brown sugar,
   packed
1 egg
1/2 c. apple juice, divided
2-1/4 c. all-purpose flour
1 t. baking soda

1/4 t. salt
1 t. cinnamon
1/4 t. ground cloves
1 c. apples, cored, peeled
   and shredded
Garnish: 5 T. walnuts,
   finely chopped

Blend together shortening and brown sugar; beat in egg and 1/4 cup
apple juice. Set aside. Combine flour, baking soda, salt and spices; add
to shortening mixture along with remaining apple juice and apples.
Drop by teaspoonfuls, 2 inches apart, onto greased baking sheets.
Bake at 350 degrees for 10 to 12 minutes, until golden. Let cool on
wire racks. Spread with Brown Sugar Frosting; sprinkle with chopped
walnuts. Makes 2 dozen.

Brown Sugar Frosting:

2 to 3 T. margarine, softened
1/3 c. light brown sugar, packed
2 T. water

1-1/2 c. powdered sugar
2 to 4 T. milk

Combine margarine, brown sugar and water in a saucepan over
medium-high heat, stirring until sugar dissolves. Remove from heat;
stir in powdered sugar and enough milk to make a spreadable
consistency. Use immediately. If frosting begins to harden,
return to low heat and stir in more milk.

Razzle-Dazzle DROP COOKIES

Gingersnaps

Carol McKinney
Poulsbo, WA

My mother told me many times when she and Daddy were first married she would make these cookies. Daddy would start eating them warm from the oven until he couldn't eat any more!

1-1/2 c. shortening
2-1/2 c. sugar, divided
2 eggs
1/2 c. molasses
4 c. all-purpose flour

2 t. baking soda
2 t. cinnamon
2 t. ground cloves
2 t. ground ginger

Blend together shortening and 2 cups sugar. Mix in eggs; add molasses and set aside. Sift together flour, baking soda and spices; add to shortening mixture and blend well. Roll into one-inch balls; roll in remaining sugar. Place 2 inches apart on baking sheets lined with parchment paper. Bake at 375 degrees for 15 to 18 minutes, watching carefully toward end of baking time. Makes about 5 dozen cookies.

There's nothing like a cookie jar full of cookies, and kids away at college will be thrilled to open a care package and find one filled with Mom's best goodies.

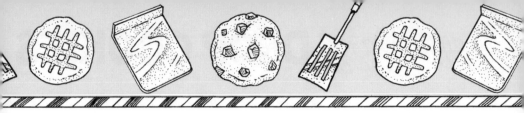

Buttery Mint Cookies

Michelle Campen
Peoria, IL

These cookies are a hit with kids of all ages! In springtime, use pastel sugars, red and blue in the summer or orange and black in the fall. These cookies always make nice gifts to give too.

3/4 c. butter
1/2 c. sugar
1 egg yolk
2 T. milk

1/4 t. mint extract
2 c. all-purpose flour
red and green colored sugars

In a mixing bowl, beat butter with an electric mixer on medium speed for 30 seconds. Add sugar; beat until combined. Beat in egg yolk, milk and extract. Add flour; blend in as much as possible with mixer. Stir in remaining flour with a wooden spoon. Cover and chill for 2 hours, or until easy to handle. Shape dough into one-inch balls; arrange on ungreased baking sheets. Dip the bottom of a glass tumbler into colored sugar and use to flatten cookies. Bake at 350 degrees for 8 to 10 minutes, or until edges begin to turn golden. Cool cookies on a wire rack. Store in an airtight container. Makes 3-1/2 dozen cookies.

Serve up cookies stacked in old-fashioned sundae glasses...what a fun after-dinner treat.

Chocolate-Peppermint Cookies

Barb Thorsen
Maple Grove, MN

The peppermint chocolate in the center of these cookies makes them irresistible!

4 1-oz. sqs. unsweetened
   baking chocolate, chopped
1 T. plus 1 t. butter, sliced
1-1/2 c. all-purpose flour
1/2 c. baking cocoa
2 t. baking powder
1/4 t. salt

4 eggs
2 c. sugar
1 t. vanilla
2 c. peppermint melting
   chocolate, chopped
Garnish: powdered sugar

Melt chocolate and butter together over low heat in a small saucepan; set aside. Stir together flour, cocoa, baking powder and salt; set aside. Combine eggs, sugar and vanilla. Mix for about 3 minutes; add chocolate mixture, then flour mixture. Mix well; cover and refrigerate for 2 hours. Shape into balls by tablespoonfuls; place 3 inches apart on parchment paper-covered baking sheets. Press 3 to 4 pieces of peppermint melting chocolate into each cookie. Bake at 325 degrees for 13 to 17 minutes. Sprinkle with powdered sugar; let cool. Makes 2-1/2 dozen.

In the end, what affects your life most deeply are the things too simple to talk about.

-Neil Blane

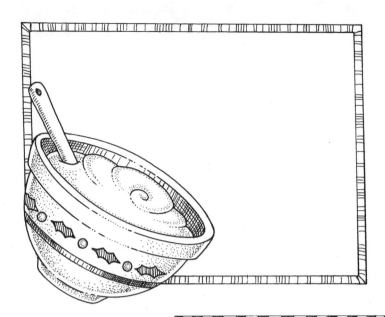

Terrific "To" "From" Tags in no time! Just copy, cut & color!

Baked with LOVE

From the Kitchen of

↑ *Cut, color & fold in half for an extra special tag.*

A Blizzard of
BAR COOKIES

Fudge Nut Bars

Nancy Molldrem
Eau Claire, WI

*When we had a neighborhood backyard potluck, my neighbor
made these bar cookies...they were a hit!*

1 c. butter, softened
2 c. light brown sugar, packed
2 eggs
2 t. vanilla extract
2 c. all-purpose flour

1 t. baking soda
1 t. salt
3 c. long-cooking oats,
    uncooked

Blend together butter and sugar; mix in eggs and vanilla and set aside.
Sift together flour, baking soda and salt; stir in oats. Add flour mixture
to butter mixture; mix well. Spread two-thirds of mixture in a greased
jelly-roll pan; cover with Chocolate Filling. Dot with remaining one-
third of mixture; swirl over filling. Bake at 350 degrees for 25 to
30 minutes; cut into 2"x1" bars. Makes 5 dozen.

Chocolate Filling:

12-oz. pkg. semi-sweet
    chocolate chips
1 c. sweetened condensed milk
2 T. butter

1/2 t. salt
2 t. vanilla extract
1 c. chopped nuts

In a saucepan over boiling water, mix
together chocolate chips, condensed milk,
butter and salt; stir until smooth. Stir in
vanilla and nuts.

Chocolate Chip Bar Cookies

Lori Hibbard
Fort Wayne, IN

These moist cookies are low in sugar...shhh, don't tell anyone!

1/2 c. butter, softened
1/2 c. light brown sugar, packed
1 egg
1 banana, mashed
1-1/2 c. all-purpose flour

1/2 t. baking soda
1/2 t. baking powder
2/3 c. mini semi-sweet
   chocolate chips
1/4 c. chopped walnuts

Blend together butter, sugar, egg and banana until smooth. Add flour, baking soda and baking powder; mix well. Stir in chocolate chips and walnuts. Spread evenly in a lightly greased 13"x9" baking pan. Bake at 350 degrees for 15 minutes or until golden. Cut into bars. Makes 2-1/2 to 3 dozen.

Marshmallow Creme Frosting

Regina Vining
Warwick, RI

Use this frosting for sandwiching cookies together...yum!

1-1/3 c. margarine, softened
7-oz. jar marshmallow creme
1 T. vanilla extract

1 t. almond extract
1 to 1-1/2 t. milk
2-2/3 c. powdered sugar

Blend margarine and marshmallow creme together until smooth; add extracts and milk and mix well. Beat in powdered sugar with an electric mixer on medium speed until smooth. Makes 3 cups.

Goodies to go...top bar cookies with frosting, then add green chocolate-covered candies in a tree or wreath shape. Fun treats for a school holiday party!

Maple Syrup Shortbread

Karen Donker
Alliance, NE

The flavor of maple paired with walnuts turns these into a real treat.

1/2 c. plus 1 T. butter, softened
   and divided
1/4 c. sugar
1 c. all-purpose flour
3/4 c. brown sugar, packed

1/2 c. maple syrup
1 egg
1 t. vanilla extract
Optional: 1/2 c. chopped walnuts

Blend 1/2 cup butter and sugar together in a large bowl until light and fluffy. Add flour a little at a time, mixing continually; blend well. Pat mixture into a lightly greased 8"x8" baking pan. Bake at 350 degrees until light golden, about 25 minutes; remove from oven and set aside. Stir together brown sugar, syrup and remaining butter. Add egg and vanilla; mix until smooth. Pour evenly over baked shortbread; sprinkle with walnuts. Return to oven; bake at 350 degrees until topping sets, about 20 minutes. Let cool; cut into 1-1/2"x1-1/2" squares. Store in an airtight container. Makes about 1-1/2 dozen.

Think outside the box...wrap cookies in clear or colored cellophane for gift giving. Tied up with a bow or curly ribbon, it's festive...fast!

Date-Nut Cookie Bars

Elizabeth Lynch
Schiller Park, IL

Sometimes I toss dried cranberries into the dough...great!

2 eggs
1/2 c. sugar
1/2 t. vanilla extract
1/2 c. all-purpose flour
1/2 t. salt

1/2 t. baking powder
1 c. walnuts
2 c. chopped dates
Garnish: powdered sugar

Beat eggs until foamy; add sugar and vanilla. Sift together flour, salt, and baking powder; stir into egg mixture. Mix in walnuts and dates; spread in a well greased 9"x9" pan. Bake at 325 degrees for 25 to 30 minutes. Cut into small squares and sprinkle with powdered sugar. Makes 1-1/2 to 2 dozen.

Hot Cocoa Nog

Leah Finks
Delaware, OH

Deliciously different...chocolatey eggnog.

2 qts. eggnog
16-oz. can chocolate syrup
Optional: 1/2 c. light rum

1 c. whipping cream
2 T. powdered sugar
Garnish: baking cocoa

Combine eggnog, chocolate syrup and rum, if desired, in a large punch bowl, stirring well. In a separate bowl, beat whipping cream with an electric mixer at high speed until foamy. Add powdered sugar and continue beating until stiff peaks form. Dollop whipped cream over eggnog; sift cocoa over top. Serve immediately. Makes 3 quarts.

Lemon-Oatmeal Bars

Carrie Kiiskila
Racine, WI

The tangy taste of lemon and orange is so refreshing.

1 c. butter, softened
1 c. sugar
2 c. all-purpose flour
1-1/4 c. long-cooking oats,
   uncooked

juice and zest of 2 lemons
juice and zest of 1 orange
14-oz. can sweetened
   condensed milk

Blend together butter and sugar. Stir in flour and oats to make a crumbly dough. Press two-thirds of dough into a greased 13"x9" baking pan; set aside. Stir juices and zests into condensed milk; spread evenly over dough in pan. Sprinkle remaining dough over top. Bake at 350 degrees for 30 to 35 minutes or until golden. When cool, cut into 2"x2" squares. Makes 2-1/2 to 3 dozen.

Here's a cookie swap table tent with a holiday feel...jot the cookie name on a piece of cardstock, then tuck the card into a pinecone.

Cream Cheese Bar Cookies

Amy Prather
Longview, WA

My mother-in-law always made these delicious cookies...now I'm carrying on the tradition.

1 c. butter, softened
1/2 c. sugar
1/2 c. cornstarch
2-1/4 c. all-purpose flour
4 eggs

16-oz. pkg. brown sugar
1/2 t. baking powder
2 t. vanilla extract
1/2 c. chopped walnuts
1/2 c. flaked coconut

Blend butter, sugar, cornstarch and 2 cups flour with a pastry blender. Pat into an ungreased jelly-roll pan; bake for 15 minutes at 350 degrees. Combine eggs, brown sugar, remaining flour, baking powder, vanilla, nuts and coconut; mix well and spread on baked layer. Bake at 350 degrees for 30 minutes. Let cool; spread with Cream Cheese Topping. Cut into bars. Makes 3-1/2 to 4 dozen.

Cream Cheese Topping:

8-oz. pkg. cream cheese, softened
1/2 c. softened butter

16-oz. pkg. powdered sugar
1 t. vanilla extract

Combine all ingredients; mix well.

Turn a simple pencil box into a sweet gift box. Covered with festive trims like colorful paper, ribbon, chenille rick-rack or buttons, in no time it's ready to fill with homebaked goodies!

Christmas Fruit Bars

*Dana Irish
Pflugerville, TX*

*These bar cookies have been one of my favorites since I was a kid.
They're easy to make and very pretty too!*

1/2 c. shortening
1-1/3 c. brown sugar, packed
1/2 t. cinnamon
1/4 t. ground cloves
1/4 t. nutmeg
2 eggs

1-1/2 c. all-purpose flour
1 t. salt
1/2 t. baking soda
2 c. candied fruit, chopped
1 c. chopped nuts

Blend together shortening, brown sugar and spices until fluffy.
Stir in eggs; set aside. Sift together flour, salt and baking soda; add to
shortening mixture. Spread evenly in a greased 13"x9" baking pan;
sprinkle fruit and nuts evenly over top. Bake at 350 degrees for
25 minutes. Cut into bars. Makes 2-1/2 to 3 dozen.

*Goodies look even more special when they're given
wrapped with care. It's easy to use fabric glue to
add simple snowflakes (cut from white felt)
onto a blue tea towel...so sweet!*

Peanut Butter Swirl Bars

Char Nix
Tustin, MI

Pairing up chocolate and peanut butter is a very good thing!

1/2 c. creamy peanut butter	2 t. vanilla extract
1/3 c. butter, softened	1 c. all-purpose flour
3/4 c. sugar	1 t. baking powder
3/4 c. brown sugar, packed	12-oz. pkg. semi-sweet
2 eggs	chocolate chips

Blend together peanut butter, butter and sugars until creamy; add eggs and vanilla. Stir in flour and baking powder; mix well. Spread in a greased 13"x9" baking pan; top with chocolate chips. Bake at 350 degrees for 5 minutes. Remove from oven; run a knife through batter to marbleize. Return to oven for an additional 30 minutes at 350 degrees. Cut into bars. Makes 2-1/2 to 3 dozen.

Easy Vanilla Frosting

Jo Ann
Gooseberry Patch

So simple, let the kids help.

2 T. egg substitute	1 t. vanilla extract
1 c. corn syrup	

Combine all ingredients in a mixing bowl; beat with an electric mixer on high speed for 6 to 7 minutes. Makes 3 cups.

Search out flea markets for tin cones to fill with sweet treats. Surprise a friend by slipping one on her door knob or add a ribbon to the cone and loop on a chair back for a clever party favor.

Chocolate-Butterscotch Bars

Debbie Isaacson
Irvine, CA

*These cookies were made by my mother for every family get-together,
and would disappear in minutes!*

12-oz. pkg. semi-sweet
   chocolate chips
12-oz. pkg. butterscotch chips
1 c. creamy peanut butter

16-oz. pkg. mini marshmallows
1 t. vanilla extract
1 c. Spanish peanuts
2 c. crispy rice cereal

Melt together chocolate chips, butterscotch chips and peanut butter in
a large saucepan over low heat. Stir in marshmallows, vanilla, peanuts
and cereal. Pour into 2 greased 8"x8" baking pans or one greased
13"x9" baking pan; press down firmly and evenly. Chill until set;
cut into small squares. Makes 2-1/2 to 3 dozen.

Cookies can be stored and still keep their
just-baked-taste for up to two weeks. Just remember
to keep them airtight...plastic zipping bags or containers
with tight-fitting lids are perfect. Even Grandma's
cookie jar will keep cookies delicious
as long as the lid is on securely.

Chocolate-Cherry Bars

Maylene Anderson
Webster City, IA

*What could possibly be better than chocolate and cherries? Make
these bars to share with friends, but keep a few for yourself too.*

18-1/2 oz. pkg. devil's food
  cake mix

21-oz. can cherry pie filling
1 t. almond extract

Mix together all ingredients; spread in a greased 13"x9" baking pan.
Bake at 350 degrees for about 25 to 35 minutes, until top springs back
when touched. Spread with Chocolate Frosting while still warm; cut
into bars. Makes 2-1/2 to 3 dozen.

Chocolate Frosting:

1 c. sugar
1/3 c. milk

5 T. margarine
1 c. semi-sweet chocolate chips

Combine sugar, milk and margarine in a saucepan. Bring to a boil; boil
for one minute, stirring constantly. Remove from heat; stir in chocolate
chips until melted.

Cookie clean-up is a
snap for bar cookies...just
line the baking pan with
aluminum foil before adding
  the dough. Once the cookies have completely cooled,
lift the cookies out, peel off the foil and cut into bars.

Eggnog Bars

Lorraine Caland
Ontario, Canada

Whenever we share these with friends, they always ask to take a few home. And more often than not, the recipe goes along too.

1/2 c. butter, softened
1 c. sugar
1 t. rum extract
2-1/4 c. all-purpose flour
1 t. baking soda

1/4 t. nutmeg
1/8 t. salt
1 c. eggnog
1 c. maraschino cherries,
   chopped

Blend together butter and sugar until fluffy; blend in extract and set aside. Combine flour, baking soda, nutmeg and salt. Add flour mixture alternately with eggnog to butter mixture; stir in cherries. Spread in a greased jelly-roll pan. Bake at 350 degrees for 18 to 20 minutes, testing for doneness with a toothpick. Drizzle with frosting while still warm. Let cool; cut into bars. Makes 4 dozen.

Frosting:

3/4 c. powdered sugar
1/2 t. rum extract
3 to 4 t. milk

Optional: several drops
   food coloring

Mix all ingredients together until smooth.

Variety is easy in cookie recipes. Finely chopped hazelnuts or macadamia nuts are a tasty substitution for walnuts in a favorite recipe.

Applesauce Spice Bars

Barbara Wise
Jamestown, OH

I found this recipe over 35 years ago on the back of a flour bag. These are the cookies my family insists I make whenever we have a family get-together.

1 c. all-purpose flour
2/3 c. brown sugar, packed
1 t. baking soda
1/2 t. salt
1 t. pumpkin pie spice

1/4 c. shortening
1 c. applesauce
1 egg
Optional: 1 c. raisins

Combine all ingredients; mix thoroughly. Spread in a greased 13"x9" baking pan. Bake for about 25 minutes at 350 degrees. Let cool; frost with Browned Butter Frosting. Cut into 3"x1" bars. Makes 2-1/2 to 3 dozen.

Browned Butter Frosting:

3 T. butter
1-1/2 c. powdered sugar

1 t. vanilla extract
1 to 1-1/2 T. milk

Heat butter in a saucepan over medium heat until it turns a delicate brown; remove from heat. Blend in remaining ingredients; beat until frosting is smooth and a spreading consistency.

A budding baker will squeal with delight to receive an apron with pockets filled to the brim with cookie cutters, jimmies, glittery sugars, frostings and tried & true recipes.

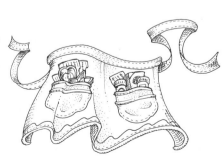

Double Bars

Julie Milliken
Lakewood, CO

All the yummy goodies in these layered bars are found in one bite.

1/2 c. margarine
1-1/2 c. graham cracker crumbs
14-oz. can sweetened
   condensed milk

12-oz. pkg. semi-sweet
   chocolate chips
1 c. peanut butter chips

Melt margarine in a 13"x9" baking pan. Spread crumbs evenly over margarine; spread condensed milk evenly over crumbs. Top with chocolate and peanut butter chips; press down firmly. Bake at 350 degrees for 25 to 30 minutes; let cool for 5 minutes and cut into bars. Makes 2-1/2 to 3 dozen.

Here are some simple high-altitude cookie baking hints: If you're above 3000 feet, decrease the baking temperature by 25 degrees and reduce the amount of sugar by 2 tablespoons per cup. If you live over 5000 feet, follow the suggestions above and also decrease the baking powder a recipe calls for by one-half.

Pumpkin Squares

Kelly Liggett
Grand Haven, MI

*Don't think of pumpkin as a fall-only treat...these are
a hit year 'round.*

4 eggs
1 c. oil
2 c. sugar
1-1/2 c. pumpkin
1/2 t. salt

1 t. baking powder
1 t. baking soda
2 t. cinnamon
2 c. all-purpose flour

Mix all ingredients together; pour into a greased jelly-roll pan. Bake at
350 degrees for 25 minutes. Cool and frost. Refrigerate for one hour
before serving. Makes 3-1/2 to 4 dozen.

Frosting:

8-oz. pkg. cream cheese,
   softened
1/2 c. plus 2 T. margarine

1-1/2 c. powdered sugar
2 t. vanilla extract
2 t. milk

Blend all ingredients together with an electric mixer on medium speed
until smooth.

*Arrange lots of yummy
bar cookies on a vintage pie
plate, then tie up with tulle.
So pretty!*

Nutmeg Squares

Debbie Reina
Houston, TX

I've been known to call my friend Nancy asking, "Do you have the nutmeg recipe? I can't find mine!" Sure enough, she does. We both simply love this crunchy cookie!

1 c. butter, softened
1 c. sugar
2 c. all-purpose flour

1-1/2 t. nutmeg
1 egg, separated

Combine butter, sugar, flour, nutmeg and egg yolk. Mix well, using hands if necessary. Pat into an ungreased jelly-roll pan; beat egg white and brush over top. Bake for one hour at 275 degrees. Let cool; cut into squares. Makes 3-1/2 to 4 dozen.

Allspice-Cream Cheese Frosting

Anna Pindell
Herrod, OH

Yum...perfect for spicy cookies.

3-oz. pkg. cream cheese
1/3 c. butter, softened
3/4 t. allspice

4 c. powdered sugar
1 t. vanilla extract
2 T. milk

Beat cream cheese, butter and allspice in a bowl with an electric mixer on medium speed until blended. Gradually add powdered sugar and blend until well combined. Stir in vanilla; gradually add milk, beating until frosting is of spreading consistency. Makes 3 cups.

Who says bar cookies can't have some extra pizazz? Dip them halfway into melted chocolate, then sprinkle with nuts or mini chips.

Peanut Butter Whimsy Bars

Erin States
Springville, PA

The kids love these after school, after play...anytime!

2 c. sugar
1/2 c. milk
1/2 c. butter
1/8 t. salt

1 t. vanilla
1/2 c. creamy peanut butter
3 c. quick-cooking oats,
  uncooked

Combine sugar, milk, butter and salt in a saucepan; bring to a boil. Boil for one minute; remove from heat. Add vanilla and peanut butter; stir until smooth. Pour over oats in a large mixing bowl; mix well. Pour mixture into a 13"x9" baking pan lined with wax paper. Allow to cool completely. Lift wax paper out of pan; cut into squares. Makes 2-1/2 to 3 dozen.

An oversize mug is perfect for filling with cookies or candy...what a terrific surprise for friends at the office!

Chinese Chews

Elaine Nichols
Mesa, AZ

*While I was growing up, Mom baked these all the time. I remember
they were so delicious with a glass of milk. Now as an adult,
I still enjoy them.*

1/2 c. shortening
1 c. sugar
2 eggs, separated
1 t. vanilla extract
1-1/2 c. all-purpose flour

1 t. baking powder
1/2 t. salt
1 c. semi-sweet chocolate chips
1 c. brown sugar, packed

Blend together shortening and sugar. Add egg yolks and vanilla; mix
well. Add flour, baking powder and salt; mix thoroughly. Press into the
bottom of a greased 13"x9" baking pan. Sprinkle with chocolate chips;
press down lightly and set aside. Beat egg whites with an electric
mixer until fluffy. Gradually add brown sugar; continue beating until
soft peaks form. Spread egg white mixture evenly over chocolate chips.
Bake at 350 degrees for 25 minutes. Let cool completely; cut into bars.
Makes 2 dozen.

*Give a cookie sampler! Just use poster board to divide
a round cookie tin into equal sections. Fill each with
a different cookie or candy...a hit!*

A Blizzard of BAR COOKIES

Chocolate-Honey Squares

Jennifer Eveland-Kupp
Temple, PA

Sure to be a hit at any gathering!

1/3 c. butter
1/2 c. baking cocoa
1/3 c. honey
3 c. mini marshmallows

1 t. vanilla extract
4 c. crispy rice cereal
1 c. peanuts

Melt butter in a large saucepan; blend in cocoa, honey and marshmallows. Cook over low heat, stirring constantly until smooth and marshmallows are melted. Remove from heat; stir in vanilla, cereal and peanuts until coated. Press lightly into a greased 9"x9" baking pan. Cut into squares when cooled. Makes 1-1/2 to 2 dozen.

Keep in mind that bar cookie dough should always
be baked in the pan size the recipe calls for.
If a larger pan size is used, the cookies will be dry.
If the pan is too small the cookies will be underbaked.

Double-Chocolate Brownies

Liz Gist
Orlando, FL

You can't stop with just one!

3 1-oz. sqs. unsweetened
   baking chocolate
6 T. butter
2/3 c. all-purpose flour
1/8 t. salt

1-1/3 c. sugar
3 eggs, beaten
1 t. vanilla extract
3/4 c. semi-sweet
   chocolate chips

Melt together unsweetened chocolate and butter in a small, heavy saucepan over low heat. Stir until smooth; remove from heat and let cool slightly. Stir together flour and salt; set aside. Gradually stir sugar into cooled chocolate mixture. Add eggs and vanilla; stir just to combine. Fold in flour mixture. Spread in an 8"x8" baking pan sprayed with non-stick vegetable spray. Sprinkle with chocolate chips; bake at 325 degrees for 30 to 35 minutes. Use a knife to spread melted chips over the surface. Let cool; cut into squares. Makes one dozen.

Just for fun, cut brownies with a round cookie cutter and stack inside an old-fashioned canning jar.

Nana's Buttermilk Brownies

Brenda Berby
Northborough, MA

Friends will love the rich taste of real homemade brownies.

1 c. margarine
1 c. water
1/3 c. baking cocoa
2 c. all-purpose flour
2 c. sugar

1 t. baking soda
1/2 t. salt
1/2 c. buttermilk
2 eggs, beaten
1-1/2 t. vanilla extract

In a saucepan, combine margarine, water and cocoa; cook until mixture comes to a boil. Remove from heat; set aside. In a bowl, stir together flour, sugar, baking soda and salt; add buttermilk, eggs and vanilla. Pour into margarine mixture; beat until well combined. Pour into a greased and floured jelly-roll pan; bake at 400 degrees for 20 minutes. Spread Chocolate-Buttermilk Frosting over the top; cut into large squares. Makes 2 dozen.

Chocolate-Buttermilk Frosting:

4 T. butter
1/4 c. baking cocoa
1/4 c. buttermilk

1 t. vanilla extract
2-1/4 c. powdered sugar

In a saucepan, combine butter, cocoa and buttermilk; bring to a boil. Remove from heat; stir in vanilla and powdered sugar.

Pineapple Bars

Phyllis Peters
Three Rivers, MI

Give these mouthwatering bars on a pretty tray all wrapped in clear cellophane. Tie with a bow and add a tag...the perfect hostess gift.

2 eggs, beaten
1-1/2 c. sugar
1 t. vanilla extract
20-oz. can crushed pineapple,
   juice reserved

2-1/4 c. all-purpose flour
1-1/2 t. baking soda
Optional: 1-1/2 c. flaked
   coconut, 1/2 c. English
   walnuts, broken up

Combine eggs, sugar and vanilla; stir in pineapple with juice, flour and baking soda, coconut and walnuts, if using. Pour into a greased jelly-roll pan; bake at 350 degrees for 20 to 25 minutes. Spread Vanilla Glaze over top while still warm; cut into bars. Makes 3 to 3-1/2 dozen.

Vanilla Glaze:

3/4 c. sugar
1/4 c. evaporated milk

1/2 c. margarine
1 t. vanilla extract

Mix all ingredients together; bring to a boil. Cook for 30 seconds.

Jams and jellies add a yummy tartness to cookies. Sandwich jam between two cookies or warm it for a simple fruity glaze.

Banana Split Bars

Carol Hickman
Kingsport, TN

The flavor of an all-time favorite dessert in a cookie!

1/3 c. butter, softened
1 c. sugar
1 egg
1 banana, mashed
1 t. vanilla extract
1-1/4 c. all-purpose flour
1 t. baking powder

1/4 t. salt
1/3 c. chopped walnuts
2 c. mini marshmallows
1 c. semi-sweet chocolate chips
1/3 c. maraschino cherries,
    quartered

Stir butter and sugar together; add egg, banana and vanilla. Stir in flour, baking powder and salt; add nuts. Pour into a greased 13"x9" baking pan; bake at 350 degrees for 20 minutes. Remove from oven; sprinkle with marshmallows, chocolate chips and cherries. Bake for an additional 10 to 15 minutes; cool. Cut into bars. Makes 2 dozen.

Fill a soda shop-style banana split bowl with Banana Split Bars...sure to get smiles!

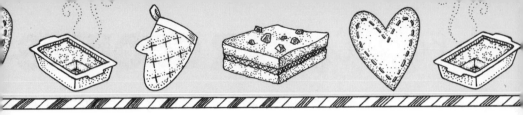

Lemon-Butter Snow Bars

Linda Hendrix
Moundville, MO

Lay a small cookie cutter over each bar before dusting with powdered sugar...so pretty.

1/2 c. butter, softened
1-1/3 c. plus 2 T. all-purpose
   flour, divided
1 c. sugar, divided
2 eggs

1/4 t. baking powder
3 T. lemon juice
1 t. lemon zest
Garnish: powdered sugar

In a medium mixing bowl, combine butter, 1-1/3 cups flour and 1/4 cup sugar. Mix on low speed for one minute with an electric mixer. Pat into an ungreased 8"x8" baking pan. Bake at 350 degrees for 15 to 20 minutes or until golden on edges. For filling, combine remaining flour, sugar, eggs, baking powder, lemon juice and lemon zest; blend well. Pour filling over partially baked crust. Bake at 350 degrees for an additional 18 to 20 minutes or until set; cool. Sprinkle with powdered sugar; cut into bars. Makes one dozen.

A lunchbox treat...pop wrapped cookies in the freezer the night before. When packing lunch in the morning, add a bag of frozen cookies to each lunchbox. They help keep the lunches cool and are ready to eat by lunchtime!

Apricot Bars

Ann Magner
New Port Richey, FL

Stack these yummy bars pyramid-style on a festive cake plate.
They won't last long.

2/3 c. dried apricots, chopped
1/2 c. butter
1/4 c. sugar
1-1/3 c. all-purpose flour,
    divided
1/2 t. baking powder

1/2 t. salt
1 c. brown sugar, packed
2 eggs
1/2 t. vanilla extract
1/2 c. chopped nuts
Garnish: powdered sugar

Cover apricots with water in a saucepan and simmer for 10 minutes; drain and set aside. Mix butter, sugar and one cup flour until crumbly. Pat into a greased 8"x8" baking pan lined with greased aluminum foil. Bake at 350 degrees for 25 minutes, or until lightly golden. Sift together remaining flour, baking powder and salt; set aside. Gradually beat brown sugar into eggs. Add flour mixture and mix well. Add vanilla, nuts and apricots. Spread over baked layer; bake an additional 30 minutes. Cool in pan; cut into squares and roll in powdered sugar. Makes one dozen.

Cookies by the pint! Fill wooden berry baskets lined with parchment paper with an assortment of cookies. Trim the paper edges with pinking shears just for zing!

Chocolate-Caramel Bars

Camille Wheeler
Buena Vista, VA

Welcome loved ones home for the holidays with freshly baked cookies...there's nothing like this aroma as they come through the door.

1-3/4 c. plus 3 T. all-purpose
   flour, divided
1-3/4 c. quick-cooking oats,
   uncooked
1 c. brown sugar, packed
1/2 t. baking soda

1/4 t. salt
1/2 c. fruit purée for baking
1/4 c. oil
1 c. semi-sweet chocolate chips
3/4 c. caramel topping

Combine 1-3/4 cups flour, oats, brown sugar, baking soda and salt. Add fruit purée and oil; stir with fork until evenly moist and crumbly. Reserve one cup for topping. Press remaining mixture evenly into bottom of a 13"x9" pan coated with non-stick vegetable spray. Bake at 350 degrees for 15 minutes. Let cool for 10 minutes; sprinkle with chocolate chips. Stir remaining flour into caramel topping; drizzle over chocolate. Sprinkle with reserved flour mixture. Bake an additional 15 minutes or until edges are golden; cool and cut into bars. Makes 3 dozen.

Tag and yard sales can turn up retro tea and coffee tins along with vintage handkerchiefs and shiny, tinsel garlands...all great for packaging.

Scotcharoos

Kelly German
Port Angeles, WA

Practically foolproof!

1 c. corn syrup
1 c. sugar
1 c. creamy peanut butter
6 to 7 c. crispy rice cereal

12-oz. pkg. semi-sweet
chocolate chips
6-oz. pkg. butterscotch chips

In a large pan, heat corn syrup and sugar over low heat; mix until dissolved. Stir in peanut butter until melted. Remove from heat and add crispy rice cereal. Mix well and press into the bottom of a greased 13"x9" pan. Sprinkle chocolate and butterscotch chips on top. Bake at 300 degrees for approximately 5 minutes to melt chocolate; spread with knife and cool. Cut into squares. Makes 2-1/2 to 3 dozen.

Don't forget icy milk is perfect with cookies!
Some dairies still sell milk in bottles, or it can be
served up in a new vintage-style milk bottle too.
What a fun "remember when" memory.

Fudge Bars

Jane Granger
Manteno, IL

Generations of kids have loved fudge...this recipe's a winner!

1 c. margarine
2 c. brown sugar, packed
2 eggs
2 t. vanilla extract
2-1/2 c. all-purpose flour
1 t. baking soda
1 t. salt

3 c. quick-cooking oats,
  uncooked
12-oz. pkg. milk chocolate chips
14-oz. can sweetened
  condensed milk
2 T. margarine
1 c. chopped walnuts

Blend together margarine and brown sugar. Add eggs and vanilla; beat
well and set aside. Mix flour, baking soda, salt and oats together. Stir
in brown sugar mixture. Pat two-thirds of oat mixture in bottom of
a greased jelly-roll pan. Melt together chocolate chips, sweetened
condensed milk and margarine; stir in walnuts. Spread fudge filling
over the oat mixture. Drop remaining one-third of oat mixture on
top of the fudge layer by teaspoonfuls. Bake at 350 degrees for
25 minutes; cut into bars. Makes 3-1/2 to 4 dozen.

Need a dusting of powdered
sugar on bar cookies, but don't
have a small strainer? Spoon
some powdered sugar into a tea
infuser and give it a shake.
It works like a charm!

Chocolatey Caramel-Pecan Bars

Kathy Grashoff
Fort Wayne, IN

Caramel and pecans are always a terrific twosome.

1/2 c. powdered sugar
1/2 c. butter, softened
1/3 c. plus 3 T. whipping cream,
    divided
1 c. all-purpose flour

24 caramels, unwrapped
2 c. pecan halves
1 t. margarine
1/2 c. milk chocolate chips

Combine powdered sugar, butter and one tablespoon whipping cream; blend well. Add flour; mix until crumbly. With floured hands, press evenly into a greased 9"x9" baking pan. Bake at 325 degrees for 15 to 20 minutes or until firm to the touch. In a medium saucepan, combine caramels and 1/3 cup whipping cream. Cook over low heat, stirring frequently, until caramels are melted and mixture is smooth. Remove from heat. Add pecans; stir well to coat. Immediately spoon over baked base; spread carefully to cover. In a small saucepan, over low heat, melt margarine and chocolate chips, stirring constantly. Stir in remaining whipping cream; drizzle over filling. Refrigerate one hour or until filling is firm. Cut into bars. Makes 2 dozen.

Spray the inside of liquid measuring cups with non-stick vegetable spray...it keeps sticky ingredients from clinging to the cup, making cleanup a snap.

Aunt Ownie's Chocolate Bars

Wendy Lee Paffenroth
Pine Island, NY

A best-loved recipe from my husband's Aunt Eleanor.

1 c. plus 2 T. butter, divided
1/2 c. brown sugar, packed
1/2 c. sugar
2 egg yolks
1 c. all-purpose flour

1 c. quick-cooking oats,
   uncooked
10-oz. chocolate bar, chopped
1/2 c. nuts, finely chopped

Blend one cup butter and sugars together. Beat in egg yolks, flour and
oats; beat well. Spread in a greased and floured 13"x9" baking pan.
Bake at 350 degrees for 20 minutes; cool for 10 minutes. Melt
chocolate bar with remaining butter; spread over top while warm.
Sprinkle with nuts; press nuts into chocolate mixture with the back
of a spoon. Cool and cut into 1"x1" bars. Makes about 4 dozen.

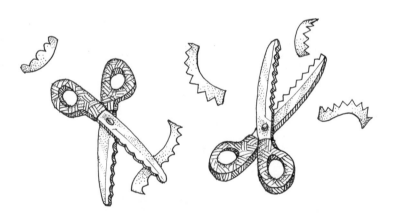

Keep a few pairs of decorative-edge scissors
on hand...terrific for adding a pretty edge
to wax, parchment or tissue paper when
wrapping up cookies to give.

Peanutty Caramel Bars

Sheila Placke
Carrollton, MO

Nothing says holidays more than trays filled with cookies that have been made with love in your own kitchen!

14-oz. pkg. caramels, unwrapped
1/4 c. water
3/4 c. creamy peanut butter, divided

4 c. doughnut-shaped oat cereal
1 c. peanuts
1 c. milk chocolate chips
1/2 c. butter, melted

Heat caramels, water and 1/2 cup peanut butter in a large saucepan until melted. Add cereal and peanuts; stir until coated. Spread into a greased 13"x9" pan. Set aside. In another pan, heat chocolate chips, butter and remaining peanut butter over low heat until melted; spread over cereal mixture. Refrigerate before cutting into bars. Makes about 3 dozen.

Photocopy family photos to use as gift tags. Just trim and secure with spray adhesive to a larger piece of cardstock. Use a hole punch in one end and slip rick-rack or a length of ribbon through the hole to tie onto a gift. A sweet tag no matter what the occasion!

To:
From:

Feel free to copy
these and use
colored pens to
give them some
ZING!

To:

FROM:

Snow
KIDDING

Carmelitas

Sally Derkenne
Des Moines, IA

For a coffee-lover, pair Carmelitas with a big bag of coffee beans and a pretty mug.

18-oz. tube refrigerated
   chocolate chip cookie dough
6-oz. pkg. semi-sweet
   chocolate chips

32 vanilla caramels, unwrapped
1/4 c. half-and-half

Slice cookie dough 1/4-inch thick; place slices in the bottom of an ungreased 9"x9" baking pan. Pat to make an even crust; bake at 375 degrees for 25 minutes. Let cool slightly; sprinkle with chocolate chips and set aside. Melt caramels and half-and-half together in a double boiler over hot water. Spread caramel mixture on top of chocolate chips. Refrigerate for one to 2 hours; cut into squares. Makes 3 dozen.

Cookie exchanges can be any time of year. Swap sweet treats on Valentine's Day, chocolatey candies at Easter or spooky shaped cut-outs on Halloween!

Peanut Butter Chipper Cookies

Tami Bowman
Marysville, OH

Store-bought sugar cookie dough means prep time for this recipe is only 5 minutes!

18-oz. tube refrigerated sugar
   cookie dough
1/2 c. creamy peanut butter
1/2 c. peanut butter chips

1/2 c. semi-sweet
   chocolate chips
1/2 c. peanuts, coarsely chopped

Blend together cookie dough and peanut butter in a large bowl until smooth. Mix in peanut butter chips, chocolate chips and nuts until evenly distributed. Drop by heaping tablespoonfuls onto ungreased baking sheets. Bake at 350 degrees for 15 minutes. Let cool slightly on baking sheets; remove to wire racks and cool. Makes 2 to 3 dozen.

Kids love cookie decorating too. Set out lots of cookies that have already been baked and cooled, then let little ones decorate them. Arrange tubes of frosting, jimmies, candies and sparkly sugars on a table and let them have fun!

"Cheesecake" Cookie Cups

Tanya Graham
Lawrenceville, GA

Wonderful cheesecake taste...no one will know your secret!

12 slices refrigerated sugar
    cookie dough
8-oz. pkg. cream cheese,
    softened
1/2 c. sweetened
    condensed milk

1 egg
1 t. vanilla extract
Optional: 21-oz. can cherry
    pie filling

Place paper liners in 12 mini muffin cups; place a slice of dough in
each cup. Bake at 325 degrees for 10 to 12 minutes, or until dough
has spread to edges of cups. Beat together cream cheese, condensed
milk, egg and vanilla in a medium bowl until smooth. Spoon about
3 tablespoons cream cheese mixture into each cookie cup. Bake for an
additional 15 to 18 minutes, or until set. Let cool completely on a wire
rack. Carefully remove cups from muffin tin. If desired, top with pie
filling. Refrigerate for one hour before serving. Makes one dozen.

Festive...fast! Arrange cookies
on a platter, then cover with
colorful plastic wrap. It comes
in lots of designs and is so
simple. Just criss-cross two long
sheets of plastic, set the platter
in the middle and gather the
ends together. Tie it all up with
ribbon, and it's ready in no time!

Cheesecake Squares

Jeanne Berfiend
Indianapolis, IN

So quick & easy...perfect for holiday baking.

2 8-oz. pkgs. cream cheese,
   softened
1 egg yolk
1 t. vanilla extract

1/2 c. sugar
2 8-oz. tubes refrigerated
   crescent rolls

Mix together cream cheese, egg yolk, vanilla and sugar until creamy;
set aside. Press one tube of crescent rolls into the bottom of a greased
13"x9" baking pan. Spoon cream cheese mixture over crescent layer;
top with remaining crescent rolls. Bake at 350 degrees for 25 minutes.
Let cool; cut into 1"x1" squares. Makes 2-1/2 to 3 dozen.

Don't forget the music! There's nothing like
cheery music in the background to really get
friends & family in the holiday spirit.

Mint Brownies

Beth Powell
Potosi, WI

*When I make these for my husband, I usually end up
only getting a small square...they go fast!*

19-1/2 oz. pkg. dark chocolate
   brownie mix
3-oz. pkg, cream cheese,
   softened
1/2 c. butter, softened

1 T. milk
1/2 t. peppermint extract
3 to 4 drops green food coloring
2 c. powdered sugar
Garnish: chocolate frosting

Prepare brownies according to package directions, using the amount
of eggs for cake-like brownies. Bake in a greased 13"x9" baking pan
according to package directions. Let cool. In a bowl, mix cream cheese
and butter until creamy. Add milk, extract, food coloring and powdered
sugar. Spread on cooled brownies; let mint layer harden. Spread with
chocolate frosting; cut into squares. Makes 2-1/2 to 3 dozen.

*Personalize gift tags to make them really special.
Write names on a pressed leaf using a gold marker,
use a paint pen on a pretty glass ornament, or
pipe frosting on bar cookies or cut-outs.*

Can't-Leave-Alone Bars

Dottie Davis
Honesdale, PA

One of my favorite recipes my daughter, Michelle, first made.
The name says it all!

18-1/4 oz. pkg. white cake mix
2 eggs
1/3 c. oil
14-oz. can sweetened
   condensed milk

6-oz. pkg. semi-sweet
   chocolate chips
1/4 c. butter, sliced

Combine dry cake mix, eggs and oil in a bowl; mix well. With floured
hands, press two-thirds of mixture into a greased 13"x9" baking pan.
Set aside. Combine condensed milk, chocolate chips and butter in a
microwave-safe bowl. Microwave, uncovered, on high setting for
45 seconds. Stir; microwave an additional 45 to 60 seconds longer
or until chips and butter are melted. Stir until smooth; pour over cake
mixture in pan. Drop remaining cake mixture by teaspoonfuls over top.
Bake at 350 degrees for 20 to 25 minutes or until light golden. Let cool
before cutting into squares. Makes 3 dozen.

Mmm...set a yummy
oversize cookie on the
top of a teacup filled
with warm, spicy tea.
The cookie keeps the tea
warm and the tea warms
up the cookie while it's
waiting to be enjoyed.

Pinwheel Cake Mix Delights

Dawn Psik
Aliquippa, PA

I LOVE these cookies! So moist and delicious, they're always popular at parties, during the holidays and especially great at bake sales. They go fast!

1/2 c. butter-flavored shortening
1/3 c. plus 1 T. butter, softened
   and divided
2 egg yolks

1/2 t. vanilla extract
18-oz. pkg. fudge marble
   cake mix, divided

Combine shortening, 1/3 cup butter, egg yolks and vanilla in a large bowl. Mix at low speed with an electric mixer until blended. Gradually add dry cake mix to shortening mixture; set aside cocoa packet from cake mix. Blend well. Divide dough into 2 portions. Add cocoa packet and remaining butter to one portion; knead until well blended and chocolate-colored. Roll out yellow dough portion between 2 pieces of wax paper into an 18"x12" rectangle, 1/8-inch thick. Repeat with chocolate dough. Remove wax paper from top of both dough portions; lay yellow dough directly on top of chocolate dough. Remove remaining wax paper; roll up jelly-roll fashion, beginning at long edge. Refrigerate for 2 hours. Cut dough into 1/8-inch slices; place on greased baking sheets. Bake at 350 degrees for 9 to 11 minutes or until lightly golden. Let cool for 5 minutes on baking sheets; remove to wire racks. Makes 3-1/2 dozen.

For a unique shape, lay cookies that are warm from the oven over a rolling pin for 2 minutes or until they take the shape.

Gingerbread Cookies, page 29

Buttermilk Sugar Cookies, page 31

Blonde Brownie Mix in a Jar, page 214

Whoopie Pies, page 56

Icebox Cookies, page 24

Chocolate Snowballs, page 55

Peanut Clusters, page 187

Chocolate-Coconut Bonbons, page 159

White Chocolate-Cranberry Cookies, page 116

White Hot Chocolate, page 45

Crisp Sugar Cookies, page 33

Hot Cocoa Nog, page 77

Teatime Tassies, page 138

Cream Cheese Cookies, page 114

Chocolate Popcorn Crunch, page 180

Super-Simple Snickerdoodles, page 123

Cowboy Cookie Mix in a Jar, page 193

Mint Brownies, page 110

Christmas Crinkle Cookies, page 53

Eggnog, page 43

Christmas Snowballs, page 158

Peanut Butter Fudge, page 170

Snow KIDDING

Red Velvet Christmas Cookies

Kathy Barnes
Elizabethton, TN

My son, Thomas, hides these from everyone because they're so good!

18-1/2 oz. pkg. red velvet cake
   mix
1/2 c. oil
2 T. water

2 eggs
12-oz. pkg. white
   chocolate chips

Combine all ingredients; mix well. Drop by tablespoonfuls onto baking sheets sprayed with non-stick vegetable spray. Bake at 350 degrees for 8 to 10 minutes. Let cool slightly before removing from baking sheets. Makes 3 dozen.

Royal Icing

Vickie
Gooseberry Patch

Ideal for decorating cookies. It dries quickly and can be tinted with food coloring too.

3 pasteurized egg whites
4-1/2 c. powdered sugar
1/2 t. cream of tartar
1/8 t. salt

Optional: 2 to 3 drops vanilla
   extract or lemon juice,
   food coloring

Beat egg whites, sugar, cream of tartar and salt with the whisk attachment of an electric mixer on medium-low speed until blended. Add vanilla or lemon juice and food coloring, if using. Increase speed to medium-high and beat until stiff peaks form and mixture is triple in volume, about 7 to 8 minutes. Cover tightly and store at room temperature for up to 6 hours. Makes 5 to 6 cups.

Tuck cookies into vellum envelopes for sweet packaging. Use decorative-edge scissors to trim the tops of the envelopes, then tie closed with a length of rick-rack.

Cream Cheese Cookies

Carol Conklin-Doggett
Shawnee, KS

Try any flavor cake mix.

1/4 c. butter, softened
8-oz. pkg. cream cheese,
  softened
1 egg

1/4 t. vanilla extract
18-1/2 oz. pkg. strawberry
  cake mix
16-oz. can strawberry frosting

Blend together butter and cream cheese; stir in egg and vanilla. Add dry cake mix one-third at a time, mixing well after each addition. Cover and chill for 30 minutes. Drop by teaspoonfuls onto ungreased baking sheets. Bake for 8 to 10 minutes at 375 degrees. Place frosting in a microwave-safe bowl. Microwave for 15 to 30 seconds; drizzle over cooled cookies. Makes 6 dozen.

Creamy Gelatin Frosting

Amy Madden
Delaware, OH

Creamy, but not too sweet.

1 c. sugar
1 T. all-purpose flour
1 T. cornstarch
1 env. unflavored gelatin
3 eggs

2 c. milk
1 T. butter
1 t. vanilla extract
1 c. heavy whipping cream,
  whipped

Combine sugar, flour, cornstarch and gelatin in a medium saucepan; mix well. Add eggs and mix until smooth; stir in milk. Cook over medium heat, stirring occasionally, until thickened, about 3 to 5 minutes. Stir in butter and vanilla. Let cool; chill until cold. Beat until smooth and fluffy. Fold whipped cream into frosting. Makes 3 cups.

Turn over vintage juice glasses and you're likely to see the prettiest patterns on the bottom. They make oh-so-pretty cookie stamps!

Crescent Pecan Pie Bars

Cheri Emery
Quincy, IL

Tastes like bite-size pecan pies!

8-oz. tube refrigerated
   crescent rolls
1 egg, beaten
1/2 c. chopped pecans

1/2 c. sugar
1/2 c. corn syrup
1 T. butter, melted
1/2 t. vanilla extract

Separate crescent dough into 2 large rectangles. Press rectangles over bottom and 1/2 inch up the sides of a lightly greased 13"x9" baking pan to form crust. Press to seal perforations in dough; bake for 5 minutes at 375 degrees. Combine remaining ingredients in a medium bowl; pour over crust. Bake an additional 18 to 22 minutes or until golden. Let cool; cut into bars. Makes 2 dozen.

Yes, there is a Mrs. Claus. She's you...busy making visions of sugarplums come true. No gift is more welcome than goodies from your own kitchen.
-Elizabeth Wood

White Chocolate-Cranberry Cookies

Sandy Bernards
Valencia, CA

Cranberries add a chewy tartness to cookie dough...a tasty treat.

18-oz. tube refrigerated white
   chocolate chunk cookie
   dough, softened
1 c. chopped pecans

3/4 c. sweetened, dried
   cranberries
1 t. orange extract
1 t. vanilla extract

Combine all ingredients; mix well. Drop by heaping teaspoonfuls,
2 to 3 inches apart, onto ungreased baking sheets. Bake for
8 to 10 minutes at 350 degrees. Makes 2 to 3 dozen.

So simple! Knead a variety of favorite chips into
store-bought sugar cookie dough, then bake.

Angel Coconut Cookies

Carla McRorie
Kannapolis, NC

Tint the coconut with food coloring if you'd like.

16-oz. pkg. angel food cake mix
1/2 c. water

1-1/2 t. almond extract
2 c. flaked coconut

MIx dry cake mix, water and extract with an electric mixer on low speed for 30 seconds. Scrape sides of bowl; mix on medium speed for one minute. Fold in coconut. Drop by rounded teaspoonfuls onto parchment paper-lined baking sheets. Bake at 350 degrees for 12 to 14 minutes. Makes 3 dozen.

Have a rubber stamp made with your initial.
Stamp it on gift bags and boxes, tissue paper
and tags...you name it!

Butterscotch Bars

Jen Burnham
Delaware, OH

Two layers of ooey, gooey butterscotch!

18-1/2 oz. pkg. butter pecan
    cake mix
1/2 c. butter, softened

1 egg
12-1/2 oz. jar caramel topping

Combine dry cake mix, butter and egg; mix well. Press half of mixture into the bottom of an ungreased 13"x9" baking pan. Bake for 10 minutes at 350 degrees. Pour caramel topping over baked crust; sprinkle with reserved cake mixture. Bake an additional 20 to 25 minutes at 350 degrees, until lightly golden; cool completely. Cut into bars. Makes 2 dozen.

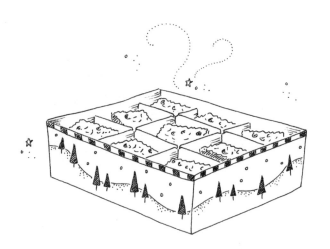

Crazy for cookies! Remind guests to bring copies of their cookie recipe along to a cookie exchange...someone's sure to ask.

Triple-Fudge Brownies

Sandi Dirickson
Anaheim, CA

I always make a double batch for my husband to take to work.
His friends say they're the best brownies they've ever tasted!

3.9-oz. pkg. instant chocolate
  pudding mix
18-1/2 oz. pkg. chocolate
  cake mix

12-oz. pkg. semi-sweet
  chocolate chips
Garnish: powdered sugar

Prepare pudding according to package directions. Whisk dry cake mix into pudding; stir in chocolate chips. Pour into a greased jelly-roll pan. Bake at 350 degrees for 30 to 35 minutes or until top springs back when lightly touched. Sprinkle with powdered sugar; cut into squares. Makes 4 dozen.

A 2 or 3-tier pie server becomes a terrific way to display cookies. Just set a plate of cookies on each tier!

Sugar Spritz Cookies

Jo Ann
Gooseberry Patch

Make it a family affair with these cookies. The dough is super easy to make and kids love using the press to make shapes.

18-oz. tube refrigerated sugar
   cookie dough, softened
several drops food coloring

Garnish: colored sugars,
   candy sprinkles

Mix cookie dough and food coloring together in a mixing bowl. If dough gets too soft, refrigerate for a few minutes. Fill cookie press with dough; press dough onto ungreased baking sheets. Decorate as desired with colored sugars and sprinkles. Bake at 325 degrees for 8 to 11 minutes, or until very lightly golden around the edges. Let cool for 2 minutes on baking sheets; remove to wire racks to finish cooling. Makes 3 dozen.

Use glass paint to share happy holiday greetings on plain glass plates. Just follow the manufacturer's easy directions to leave whimsical greetings that will be hidden under your stacks of cookies. What a surprise when all the cookies are gone!

Chocolate-Dipped Almond Cookies

Audrey Lett
Newark, DE

These are ready in a jiffy, but look like you spent hours in the kitchen.

18-oz. tube refrigerated sugar
   cookie dough, softened
1/2 c. chopped almonds

6-oz. pkg. semi-sweet
   chocolate chips

Blend together cookie dough and almonds in a medium bowl; chill for 15 minutes. Form into 1-1/2 inch balls; place on ungreased baking sheets. Bake at 325 degrees for 15 to 17 minutes, or until lightly golden around edges. Let cool on baking sheets for 2 minutes; cool completely on wire racks. Microwave chocolate chips in a small microwave-safe bowl on high setting for one minute; stir. Microwave at additional 10 to 20-second intervals, stirring until smooth. Dip cookies halfway into melted chocolate; shake off excess and place on wax paper-lined baking sheets. Chill for 15 minutes or until set. Makes 8.

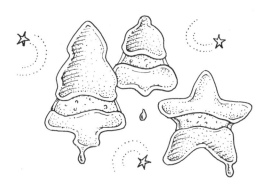

For a fun twist when dipping cookies in melted chocolate, use two types of chips for dipping. Dip cookies halfway in white chocolate and set aside. When the chocolate has cooled, turn the cookies halfway again and dip into semi-sweet chocolate...yum!

Pumpkin-Chocolate Chip Cookies

Jenn Fremming
Rexburg, ID

Out-of-this-world cookies!

18-1/2 oz. pkg. spice cake mix
15-oz. can pumpkin

6-oz. pkg. semi-sweet
chocolate chips

Combine ingredients and mix well. Drop by teaspoonfuls onto ungreased baking sheets. Bake for 14 minutes at 375 degrees. Makes about 3 dozen.

Buttermilk Frosting

Brenda Derby
Northborough, MA

An old-fashioned favorite that will be around for generations.

1 c. sugar
1/2 t. baking soda
1 c. buttermilk

1/2 t. vanilla extract
1/2 c. butter

Combine all ingredients in a large, heavy saucepan. Cook over medium heat for about 20 minutes, stirring constantly, until mixture reaches soft-ball stage, or 234 to 243 degrees on a candy thermometer. Remove pan from heat and cool for 5 minutes, then beat until it starts to thicken. Pour over top of cookies. Makes about 2-1/2 cups.

If cookies have been frozen ahead of time, it's a snap to make them taste fresh-baked in minutes. Place frozen cookies on a baking sheet and warm in a 300-degree oven for 3 to 5 minutes.

Super-Simple Snickerdoodles

Brandi Divine
Garland, TX

Kids giggle over the name, but love the taste!

18-1/2 oz. pkg. yellow cake mix
2 eggs
1/2 c. oil
1 T. cinnamon
Garnish: cinnamon-sugar

Combine cake mix, eggs, oil and cinnamon in a large bowl; mix well. Drop by teaspoonfuls onto ungreased baking sheets. Bake at 350 degrees for 8 to 10 minutes. While still warm, sprinkle with cinnamon-sugar. Let cool for 2 minutes on baking sheets; transfer to wire racks to finish cooling. Makes about 2 dozen.

Maple Frosting

Stephanie Mayer
Portsmouth, VA

Ideal for a simple butter or cut-out cookie.

1/4 c. butter
3 c. powdered sugar, divided
3 T milk
1 t. maple flavoring

Beat butter with an electric mixer on medium speed for 30 seconds. Gradually add 1-1/2 cups powdered sugar, beating well. Beat in milk and maple flavoring; gradually add remaining powdered sugar and beat to a spreadable consistency. Makes about 3-1/2 cups.

Try something new...sprinkle frosted cookies with crushed candy, chopped nuts or dried fruit, or roll drop cookies in crushed nuts before baking. Candied fruit and edible flowers, such as rose petals and violets, make beautiful cookie toppers too.

Pineapple Macaroons

Mary Patenaude
Griswold, CT

The sherbet is the secret in these fruity cookies. Try any favorite flavor sherbet for a brand-new cookie taste.

1 pt. pineapple sherbet, softened
2 t. almond extract

18-1/4 oz. pkg. white cake mix
6 c. flaked coconut

Combine sherbet, extract and cake mix; stir in coconut. Drop by tablespoonfuls, 2 inches apart, on greased baking sheets. Bake at 350 degrees for 12 to 15 minutes. Let cool on wire racks. Makes about 6 dozen.

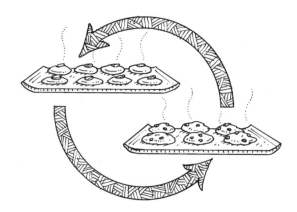

Do you have 2 baking sheets filled with cookie dough in the oven at one time? If so, remember halfway through the baking time to reverse the top and bottom sheets and turn them around.

Butterscotch Yummies

Tammy Rowe
Bellevue, OH

*Pass these around and everyone will think
you've made a visit to the bakery!*

2 c. milk
3.4-oz. box instant butterscotch
   pudding mix

18-1/4 oz. pkg. yellow cake mix
11-oz. pkg. butterscotch chips

Combine milk and pudding mix; blend in cake mix. Fold in butterscotch
chips. Spread into a jelly-roll pan sprayed with non-stick cooking
spray. Bake at 350 degrees for 30 minutes. Let cool; cut into squares.
Makes 2 dozen.

Nestle wrapped cookies inside colorful party hats and
arrange the hats in a festive bowl. A clever way to
display cookies for a cookie swap!

Fast & Fabulous Cookies

Michelle Barbaro
Clayton, NJ

*An irresistable cookie combination of cake and
white chocolate chips.*

18-1/4 oz. pkg. yellow or
   devil's food cake mix
1/2 c. water
1/4 c. butter, softened

1 egg
1 c. white chocolate chips
Optional: 1/2 c. chopped walnuts

Combine cake mix, water, butter and egg in a large mixing bowl. Beat
with mixer on low speed until moist. Increase speed to medium; beat
one minute until batter is thick. Stir in chips and nuts, if using; mix
until well blended. Drop by heaping teaspoonfuls 2 inches apart on
greased baking sheets. Bake at 350 degrees for 10 to 12 minutes or
until set. Let cookies cool on sheets for one minute; remove to a wire
rack and continue cooling. Makes 2 to 3 dozen.

Add a few curls of orange zest on frosted cookies
or brownies for a sweet & tangy taste.

Double-Chocolate Cookie Bars

Leslie Stimez
Caruthersville, MO

These extra chocolatey bars may not make it to your cookie swap!

24 chocolate sandwich cookies,
   divided
1/4 c. butter, melted
2 c. semi-sweet chocolate chips,
   divided

14-oz. can sweetened
   condensed milk
1 t. vanilla extract

Crush all except 6 sandwich cookies in a food processor or blender to a fine crumb consistency. Transfer to a small bowl; add butter and mix well. Press into the bottom of a 13"x9" pan; set aside. Combine one cup chocolate chips, condensed milk and vanilla in a microwave-safe bowl. Heat on high setting for 30 seconds at a time, stirring between each interval, until melted and smooth. Spread evenly over crumb crust. Sprinkle remaining chocolate chips over top; crush remaining cookies by hand and sprinkle over chocolate chips. Bake at 325 degrees for 20 to 25 minutes. Chill completely before cutting into bars. Makes 20 bars.

Happy Holidays

Wrap cookies with personalized ribbon! Press alphabet stamps onto an ink pad made especially for fabric. Lay a matte-finish ribbon on paper towels and stamp on a greeting, name or special date.

TO:

FROM:

To:

From:

Use our labels on your goodies!

with Love :

Take these labels to a copy machine and run some copies. Cut them out, color them with markers & tie 'em on.

Sugarplum-Perfect
COOKIES

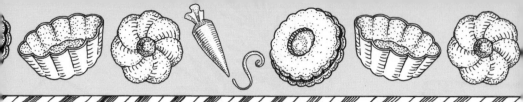

Almond Crescents

Darleen Veal
Sandersville, GA

Easy to shape into the prettiest cookies.

1 c. margarine, softened
1/2 t. almond extract
3/4 c. powdered sugar
2 c. all-purpose flour
1/2 t. salt

1 c. quick-cooking oats,
   uncooked
1/2 c. toasted almonds,
   finely chopped
Garnish: powdered sugar

Blend together margarine and extract until fluffy; gradually beat in sugar and set aside. Combine flour and salt; add to margarine mixture. Mix well. Stir in oats and almonds. Shape dough by hand into crescents; arrange on ungreased baking sheets. Bake at 325 degrees until lightly golden, 15 to 18 minutes. Roll in powdered sugar. Makes about 2 dozen.

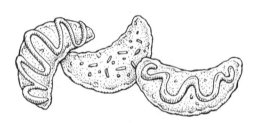

Gaufrettes

Lisa Gregos
Burbank, CA

My mother made so many of these at Christmas, she had to store them in a gigantic pickle jar!

2 c. butter, softened
6 c. all-purpose flour
2 c. sugar

2 c. brown sugar, packed
6 eggs
1 t. vanilla extract

Combine all ingredients in a large mixing bowl; stir well. Drop by heaping teaspoonfuls onto a heated waffle iron; bake according to manufacturer's instructions. Makes 3 to 4 dozen.

Sugarplum-Perfect **COOKIES**

Great-Grandma's Rum Cookies

Marybeth Gabauer
Roeland Park, KS

My grandma and I made these cookies at Thanksgiving and Christmas every year. I have continued the tradition with my own daughter.

1 c. butter, softened
2 t. vanilla extract
1 t. rum extract
3/4 c. sugar

1 egg, beaten
3 c. all-purpose flour
1 t. nutmeg

Combine butter with extracts. Gradually add sugar; blend well. Add egg; beat mixture and set aside. Sift flour and nutmeg together; slowly add to butter mixture. Roll out dough 1/2-inch thick on a floured surface; cut into 3-inch pieces Place on ungreased baking sheets; bake for 13 to 15 minutes at 350 degrees. Let cool; frost with Rum Frosting. Makes 5 to 6 dozen.

Rum Frosting:

1/2 t. vanilla extract
1 T. rum extract
3 T. butter, softened

2-1/2 c. powdered sugar
2 to 3 T. milk or half-and-half

Blend extracts into butter; mix until creamy. Stir in sugar; add milk or half-and-half one tablespoon at a time until frosting is at desired consistency.

Try something new when serving coffee with cookies. For a rich flavor, try Coffee Creole...just add 1/2 teaspoon of molasses to each cup of coffee.

Krumkake

Jennifer Williams
Burnsville, MN

This cookie recipe was handed down from my Great-Aunt Minnie and when I make them, I think of my Danish heritage. They are beautifully patterned with a design imprinted on the krumkake iron and can be served plain, dusted with sugar, dipped in chocolate or rolled into a cone and filled with whipped cream or ice cream!

3 eggs
1 c. sugar
1/2 c. butter, melted

1/2 t. nutmeg
1/2 c. whipping cream, whipped
2 c. all-purpose flour

Beat eggs until very light; stir in sugar, butter, nutmeg and cream. Add enough flour to handle easily. Place one teaspoonful of dough on a heated krumkake iron; bake according to manufacturer's instructions until very lightly golden. Roll quickly around krumkake pin. Store in an airtight container. Makes about 2 dozen.

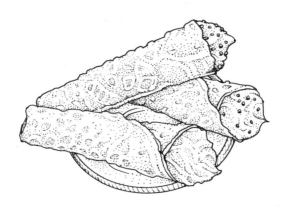

Tag making is easy...just dress up a mailing tag with a little ribbon, rub on letters and a pretty posy. Great for gift giving or to let friends know what type of yummy cookie you've brought to share!

Sugarplum-Perfect COOKIES

Mom's Italian Biscotti

Jeanette Toscano
Pomona, NY

My parents immigrated from Italy in the 1960s and brought this biscotti recipe with them. These cookies have a buttery-light texture with a hint of lemon sweetness. On Christmas Eve, children of all ages look forward to dunking them in milk, coffee or tea.

5-1/2 c. all-purpose flour	6 eggs
1 T. plus 2 t. baking powder	zest and juice of 2 lemons
3/4 c. butter, softened	3-1/2 c. powdered sugar
1-1/2 c. sugar	

Mix together flour, baking powder, butter and sugar; form a well in the center. Add eggs and zest; knead until dough is smooth. Shape dough into 2-inch balls on a floured surface; roll each into a 7-inch rope. Twist into knots; place on lightly greased baking sheets. Bake at 350 degrees for 15 to 18 minutes. Cool on a wire rack. Combine lemon juice and powdered sugar; drizzle over cookies. Makes 3 dozen.

Cookie swap fun! Hand out raffle tickets as friends arrive and raffle off cookie cutters, ornaments, bubble night lights or candles.

Holiday Butter Tarts

Julie Ehrman
International Falls, MN

These tarts are deliciously simple to prepare!

1 c. butter, softened
2 3-oz. pkgs. cream cheese,
   softened

2 c. all-purpose flour

Blend together butter and cream cheese; stir in flour. Cover and chill about one hour or until easy to handle. Shape into 1-3/4 inch balls; press into bottoms and up sides of ungreased muffin cups. Fill each with about one heaping teaspoon of butter tart filling. Bake at 425 degrees for 8 to 10 minutes; reduce heat to 350 degrees and bake for an additional 10 minutes. Cool slightly in muffin cups; remove and cool well. Makes 4 dozen.

Butter Tart Filling:

2 eggs
2 c. brown sugar, packed
2/3 c. butter, melted
1/4 c. evaporated milk

1 t. vanilla extract
4 t. all-purpose flour
1 c. raisins

Beat together eggs, brown sugar and butter in a small bowl. Stir in evaporated milk, vanilla, flour and raisins.

Be sure to find out if there are special stories or sweet memories behind the recipes brought, then ask friends to share the memory.

Sugarplum-Perfect COOKIES

Waffle Cookies

Donna Schloemer
Tacoma, WA

Made on a waffle iron!

4 1-oz. sqs. unsweetened baking chocolate	1-1/2 c. sugar
1 c. margarine	2 c. all-purpose flour
4 eggs	2 t. vanilla extract

Melt together chocolate and margarine in a saucepan over low heat; remove from heat. Add eggs, sugar, flour and vanilla; mix well. Drop by teaspoonfuls onto a heated waffle iron; bake according to manufacturer's instructions. Frost with chocolate frosting. Makes 2 dozen.

Chocolate Frosting:

2 1-oz. sqs. unsweetened baking chocolate	4 T. milk
1/4 c. margarine	2 t. vanilla extract
	2-1/2 to 3 c. powdered sugar

Melt together chocolate and margarine in a saucepan over low heat; remove from heat and add milk and vanilla. Mix in powdered sugar to desired consistency.

Tote cookies to the party stacked in the bed of a vintage-style toy truck...how clever!

Bite-Size Jam Swirls

Pat Habiger
Spearville, KS

I think these are so pretty, light and tasty with butter and cream cheese. They take a little time, but are well worth it!

3 c. all-purpose flour
1/8 t. salt
8-oz. pkg. cream cheese,
   softened

1 c. butter, softened
1/2 c. raspberry jam
1 c. finely chopped walnuts
Garnish: coarse sugar

Combine flour and salt in a medium mixing bowl. Using a pastry blender, cut in cream cheese and butter until mixture resembles fine crumbs and begins to cling together. Divide dough in half; cover and chill for one hour. On a lightly floured surface, roll each half of dough to 1/4-inch thickness. Fold each half into thirds, wrap in plastic wrap and chill for 2 hours. Roll each half of dough out on a floured surface to a 14"x12" rectangle. Spread each rectangle with jam to 1/2 inch from edges; sprinkle with nuts. Beginning with long side, roll up jelly-roll style; seal seam. Cut into 1/2-inch thick slices; dip one side of each slice in sugar. Arrange one inch apart on ungreased baking sheets. Bake at 375 degrees for about 15 minutes or until lightly golden. Remove from baking sheets; cool on a wire rack. Makes 3 dozen.

Pipe icing on cookies so they look like tiny, tasty presents!

Sandbakkels

Stacey Weichert
Waseca, MN

One of my earliest memories is a Christmas when I was just 4 years old. Christmas baking was in full force with Mom, Grandma and Great Grandma Sunny. They all wore pretty homemade aprons and I remember my sisters and I wanted to wear aprons too. Grandma would grab pins and big white flour sack dish towels, then pin them around us. Mine went all the way to the floor! The goodies were endless, but the Sandbakkels, a Norwegian cookie, were my favorite.

1 c. butter, softened	1 t. almond extract
1 c. sugar	2-1/2 c. all-purpose flour
1 egg	

Blend together butter and sugar; add egg and extract. Add flour to make a stiff dough. Press as thin as possible into greased sandbakkel tins or small tartlet pans. Bake at 350 degrees for 15 minutes or until lightly golden. Let cool slightly, then tap out of tins. Makes about 3-1/2 dozen.

Cookie recipe booklets are a cookie-exchange favorite! A few days before the party, ask friends to share their recipes. Then, make copies and put them together in a booklet for everyone to take home.

Teatime Tassies

Linda Behling
Cecil, PA

*This recipe takes me back to my childhood Christmases. My mom
made them every year, now I do the same for my children,
grandchildren and friends.*

3-oz. pkg. cream cheese,
  softened
1/2 c. butter, softened
1 c. all-purpose flour

1 egg, beaten
3/4 c. brown sugar, packed
1 t. vanilla extract
3/4 c. finely chopped nuts

Blend together cream cheese and butter; stir in flour and mix well.
Refrigerate for about 30 minutes. Divide dough into 24 balls; press
into greased mini muffin cups. Combine egg, brown sugar, vanilla and
nuts; fill cups 3/4 full. Bake at 325 degrees for 25 to 30 minutes or
until golden. Let cool 5 minutes before removing from cups. Makes
2 dozen.

Set out a variety of beverages to make cookie nibbling
more fun. Flavorful coffees, teas, fruity punches and,
of course, ice-cold milk are perfect.

Strawberry Cookies

Heather Rulli
Gurnee, IL

My mother and I have made these cookies together ever since I was a little girl.

1/4 c. margarine	1-1/2 c. crispy rice cereal
1-1/3 c. chopped dates	1/2 c. finely chopped walnuts
1/2 c. flaked coconut	1 T. vanilla extract
1/2 c. sugar	Garnish: red sugar, tube of
1 egg, beaten	green frosting
1/8 t. salt	

Melt margarine in a Dutch oven; add dates, coconut, sugar, egg and salt. Stir thoroughly. Cook over low heat until mixture thickens and bubbles, 5 to 10 minutes. Remove from heat; stir in cereal, nuts and vanilla. Let cool for 10 minutes. Spray hands with non-stick vegetable spray. Form about a tablespoon of warm mixture into a strawberry shape; roll in red sugar. Repeat with remaining mixture. Use green frosting to make a leaf shape on top of each "strawberry." Let dry. Makes about 4 dozen.

Vintage sand pails, new paint cans, retro-style lunch-boxes and cowboy hats are just a few containers you can use to display cookies for an exchange. It's all about having fun!

Fruit-Filled Spritz

Elaine Nichols
Mesa, AZ

I think these are just the best holiday cookie!

1 c. butter, softened
1 c. sugar
1/2 c. brown sugar, packed
3 eggs
1/2 t. almond extract
1/2 t. vanilla extract
4 c. all-purpose flour
1/2 t. baking soda
1/2 t. salt
Garnish: powdered sugar

Combine butter and sugars in a mixing bowl; blend well. Beat in eggs and extracts; set aside. Combine flour, baking soda and salt; add gradually to butter mixture. Use a cookie press fitted with a bar disk to press a 12-inch strip of dough onto ungreased baking sheets. Spread fruit filling over dough; press another strip over filling. Cut into one-inch pieces; do not separate the pieces. Repeat with remaining dough and filling. Bake at 375 degrees for 12 to 15 minutes or until edges are golden. Recut into pieces if necessary; remove to wire racks to cool. Sprinkle with powdered sugar. Makes 7-1/2 dozen.

Fruit Filling:

1-1/2 c. chopped dates
1 c. water
1/2 c. sugar
2 t. orange juice
2 t. orange zest
1 c. maraschino cherries, chopped
1/2 c. flaked coconut
1/2 c. ground nuts

Combine dates, water, sugar, orange juice and zest in a saucepan. Bring to a boil, stirring constantly. Reduce heat; cook and stir for 8 minutes or until thickened. Let cool completely. Stir in cherries, coconut and nuts.

Sugarplum-Perfect COOKIES

Springerle

April Hale
Kirkwood, NY

This cookie may seem hard to make, but it's not! I make them every year for my family…they're yummy!

4 c. all-purpose flour
1 t. baking powder
1/2 t. salt
4 eggs

2 c. sugar
1/8 t. anise extract
2 t. lemon zest
powdered sugar

Sift flour, baking powder and salt together; set aside. In a large bowl, mix eggs with an electric mixer at high speed until thick and lemon colored, about 5 minutes. At medium speed, gradually add sugar 2 tablespoons at a time; add extract. Add flour mixture to egg mixture and zest; mix well until smooth. Sprinkle powdered sugar on a springerle rolling pin and pastry cloth or wooden board. Slowly roll springerle pin over dough to make designs; cut dough along lines to make individual cookies. Place on lightly greased baking sheets. Bake at 325 for 15 minutes or just until lightly golden. Makes about 4 dozen.

Flea markets and tag sales are ideal places to spot bargains on old-fashioned cookie presses and springerle rolling pins.

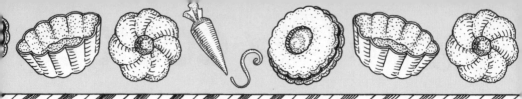

Butter Tarts

Irene O'Donnell
Moline, IL

A Canadian recipe handed down from my mother-in-law.
It's a real family favorite.

2 c. cake flour
1/3 t. salt
2/3 c. shortening

2 T. brown sugar, packed
3-1/2 T. cold water

Sift together flour and salt; cut in shortening and brown sugar.
Gradually sprinkle with water; mix lightly. Form into a ball; roll to a
16"x12" rectangle on a floured surface. Using a 4" round cutter, cut
into 12 circles. Press each circle of dough into a greased tart tin or
muffin cups. Fill two-thirds full with raisin filling. Bake for 15 to
18 minutes at 375 degrees. Makes one dozen.

Raisin Filling:

1/2 c. raisins
1/4 c. butter
1/2 c. brown sugar, packed
1/2 c. corn syrup

1 egg, beaten
1/4 t. salt
1/2 t. vanilla extract

Cover raisins with boiling water; let stand for 10 minutes. Blend butter
and brown sugar; add remaining ingredients. Drain raisins; stir into
butter mixture.

Cookies are made of
butter and love.
-Norwegian Proverb

Lady Locks

Sandra Reisner
Cedar Rapids, IA

These fun cookies are made using clothespins!

3 c. all-purpose flour
1 c. sour cream

1-1/2 c. butter, softened
Garnish: powdered sugar

Wrap several round wooden clothespins or 5-inch dowels with aluminum foil; set aside. Combine flour, sour cream and butter; blend well. Divide into 8 portions; chill overnight. For each dough portion, roll in powdered sugar, then roll out to a 6"x4" rectangle, 1/8-inch thick, on a powdered sugar-covered surface. Cut dough into 4"x1" strips; wrap each strip spiral-fashion, overlapping, around a clothespin. Arrange on ungreased baking sheets; bake at 350 degrees for 10 to 20 minutes, until slightly golden. Immediately remove from baking sheets to a wire rack. Slide cookies off clothespins as soon as possible using a gentle twisting motion and return to wire rack. Let cool; pipe filling into cookies. Sprinkle with powdered sugar, if desired. Makes about 4 dozen.

Filling:

5 T. all-purpose flour
1-1/2 c. milk
3/4 c. butter, softened

3/4 c. shortening
1-1/2 c. sugar
3/4 t. vanilla extract

Combine flour and milk in a saucepan; bring to a boil until mixture thickens. Let cool. Combine butter, shortening, sugar and vanilla; mix well. Add cooled flour mixture a little at a time; mix well for 8 minutes.

Christmas Tassies

Mary Lou Sewell
Milford, CT

These are my daughter's Christmas treat every year.

1/2 c. plus 1 T. butter, softened
   and divided
3-oz. pkg. cream cheese,
   softened
3 T. sugar
1/2 t. vanilla extract
1 c. all-purpose flour

1/4 c. finely ground almonds
4 T. raspberry jam
2 1-oz. sqs. semi-sweet
   baking chocolate
Garnish: colored sugars,
   candy sprinkles

Beat together 1/2 cup butter, cream cheese, sugar and vanilla until fluffy. Add flour and almonds; stir until well blended. Wrap dough in plastic wrap and refrigerate overnight. Divide dough into 24 portions; gently press into the bottoms and sides of ungreased mini muffin cups to form shells. Bake for 13 minutes at 350 degrees. Let cool slightly; loosen with a small knife to remove from cups. When completely cooled, spoon 1/2 teaspoon raspberry jam into each shell. Melt together chocolate and remaining butter in a small saucepan over hot (not boiling) water. Spoon a dollop of chocolate onto jam. Refrigerate until chocolate sets; decorate tops as desired. Makes 2 dozen.

Dress up invitations with sparkly glitter pens, rubber stamps, stickers, ribbon, rick-rack or buttons...make them festive and fun!

Victorian Stamped Cookies

Kathy Grashoff
Fort Wayne, IN

The perfect dough for pressing with a cookie stamp.

3/4 c. butter, softened
3/4 c. brown sugar, packed
1 egg
1 t. vanilla extract

1/2 t. butter extract
2-1/4 c. all-purpose flour
1/8 t. salt

Blend together butter and sugar in a large bowl until creamy. Add egg and extracts; beat until smooth and set aside. Combine flour and salt; add to butter mixture and stir well. Chill for one hour. Shape into one-inch balls; place 2 inches apart on greased baking sheets. Flatten balls with 2" round cookie stamps. Bake at 350 degrees for 9 to 11 minutes or until bottoms are golden. Transfer to a wire rack to cool; store in an airtight container. Makes 5 dozen.

Tie an invitation onto individually wrapped cookies or cookies slipped into a vellum bag. Hand deliver to friends for an oh-so-tasty invitation!

Candy-Cane Cookies

Kelly Simpson
Rapid City, SD

So festive...tuck into stockings for a Christmas morning surprise.

1 c. sugar	1 t. almond extract
2/3 c. margarine, softened	3 c. all-purpose flour
1/2 c. egg substitute	1 t. baking powder
2 t. vanilla extract	1/2 t. red food coloring

Beat together sugar and margarine until creamy with an electric mixer at medium speed. Beat in egg substitute and extracts; set aside. Mix flour and baking powder; stir into margarine mixture. Divide dough in halves; tint one half with food coloring. Wrap separately; refrigerate for 2 hours. Divide each half into 32 pieces; roll each into a 5-inch rope. Twist together one red and one plain rope and bend end to form candy canes. Place on ungreased baking sheets. Bake at 350 degrees for 8 to 10 minutes, until golden. Remove from baking sheets; cool on wire racks. Store in an airtight container. Makes 2-1/2 dozen.

Arrange tall goodies, like Candy Cane Cookies, in a pretty parfait glass...it's just the right size and shape.

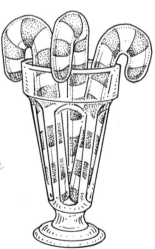

Chocolate Waffle Cookies

Toni Smith
Monroe, UT

Kids big and little will love this chocolatey cookie!

2 1-oz. sqs. unsweetened
    baking chocolate
1/2 c. butter
2 eggs, beaten

3/4 c. sugar
1 c. all-purpose flour
1 t. vanilla extract
1/2 c. chopped nuts

Melt together chocolate and butter in a saucepan over low heat; let cool for 2 minutes. Add remaining ingredients; mix well. Drop by teaspoonfuls, about 4 at a time, onto a heated waffle iron at medium setting. Close lid; bake for one minute. Makes one dozen.

Give your cookie swap a theme...Chocolate Only, Old-Fashioned Favorites or The Gingerbread Man. Use the same theme to make choosing invitations and decorating a snap.

Tootie Fruity Cookies

Paula Schultz
West St. Paul, MN

*I also make these cookies into tiny ice cream sandwiches.
Put a scoop of frozen yogurt or sherbet between 2 of them.*

1/2 c. shortening	1 t. vanilla extract
1/4 c. margarine, softened	2-1/2 c. all-purpose flour
3-oz. pkg. fruit flavor	1 t. baking powder
gelatin mix	1 t. salt
1/2 c. sugar	Garnish: sugar
2 eggs	

Mix together shortening, margarine, gelatin mix, sugar, eggs and
vanilla. Stir in remaining ingredients; form into one-inch balls and
roll in extra sugar. Place 3 inches apart on ungreased baking sheets;
flatten with cookie stamps dipped in sugar. Bake for 6 to 8 minutes
at 400 degrees. Makes about 5 dozen.

A warm & cozy hostess
gift...cocoa mixes tucked inside
a new pair of mittens or
a coffee mix slipped inside
a thermos.

Strasbourg Cookies

LaVerne Fang
Delavan, IL

Try this with your favorite flavor of jelly.

1 c. butter, softened
1/2 c. powdered sugar
1 t. vanilla extract

2-1/2 c. all-purpose flour
1/4 c. strawberry, raspberry or
   grape jelly

Blend butter, sugar and vanilla; gradually stir in flour until well blended. Let stand 30 minutes. Press dough through a star piping tip onto lightly greased baking sheets, making rosettes one inch apart. Make a small indentation in center of each; fill with a dollop of jelly. Bake at 325 degrees for 15 minutes, until set and golden. Makes 3 to 4 dozen.

What teacher wouldn't love an old-fashioned
lunchbox filled with cookies and brownies?
A sweet way to say "Thank you."

Pizzelles

Vickie
Gooseberry Patch

A thin, wafer-like cookie with an anise taste.

6 eggs, beaten
1-1/2 c. sugar
1 c. margarine, melted
   and cooled

2 T. anise extract
3-1/2 c. all-purpose flour
4 t. baking powder

Place eggs in a bowl; gradually beat in sugar until smooth. Add margarine and anise extract; mix well. Gradually mix in flour and baking powder; dough will be sticky enough to drop rounded teaspoonfuls onto a heated pizzelle iron. Bake according to manufacturer's instructions. Makes 3 dozen.

Christmas Punch

Betty Adams
Canal Winchester, OH

Add cranberries and lemon curls to your ice ring
before freezing...so pretty when you float it in the punch bowl.

3 12-oz. cans frozen orange
   juice concentrate
1-1/2 c. light corn syrup

5 qts. ginger ale, chilled
1/4 c. lime juice
Garnish: ice ring

Combine orange juice, corn syrup and lime juice in a punch bowl; mix thoroughly. Just before serving, add ginger ale and ice ring. Makes about 5-1/2 quarts.

Sweets for a sweetie...pipe
chocolatey x's and o's
on top of cookies before
giving to someone special.
Sure to be a hit!

Sugarplum-Perfect COOKIES

Double Chocolate-Almond Biscotti

Lisa Ashton
Aston, PA

Handed down from my Italian mom who loves to bake.

2 c. all-purpose flour	2 eggs
1/2 c. baking cocoa	1 t. vanilla extract
1-1/2 t. baking powder	1/2 t. almond extract
1/2 t. salt	1 c. almonds, coarsely chopped
1/2 c. butter, softened	2/3 c. semi-sweet
1-1/4 c. sugar	chocolate chips

Combine flour, cocoa, baking powder and salt; set aside. Blend butter and sugar until light and fluffy; beat in eggs and extracts. Gradually blend in flour mixture; stir in almonds and chocolate chips. Shape dough into 2 logs about 15"x1-1/2"; place about 3 inches apart on parchment paper-lined baking sheets. Bake at 325 degrees until edges start to turn golden and top becomes firm, about 50 to 55 minutes. Remove from oven; let cool. Cut into 1/2-inch diagonal slices. Place slices cut-side down on baking sheets; lower oven to 275 degrees and bake an additional 20 minutes until dried. Makes 4 dozen.

There's no easier gift bag than a classic brown paper lunch sack. Fill with treats, fold the top over, punch 2 holes and slide a peppermint stick or candy cane through. You could even thread a licorice whip through the holes and tie into a bow!

Peanut Butter Cup Tarts

Ann Fehr
Trappe, PA

Try using chocolate dough too...a recipe that just can't miss.

18-oz. tube refrigerated peanut
    butter cookie dough

36 mini peanut butter cups,
    unwrapped

Slice dough 3/4-inch thick; cut each slice into quarters. Place each
piece of dough in a greased mini muffin cup. Bake at 350 degrees
for 8 to 10 minutes, or just until cookies puff. Remove from oven;
immediately push a peanut butter cup into each cookie. Let cool
until pan is cold; refrigerate until chocolate is no longer shiny.
Gently remove cookies, using a knife if necessary. Makes 3 dozen.

Remember those great vintage candle sets...carolers,
reindeer, Santa and snowmen? They can still be
found today at tag sales or antique shops.
March them right down the center of the cookie
table for a very nostalgic feel.

Chocolate-Cream Macaroon Tarts

Melanie Lowe
Dover, DE

These muffin-cup size tarts are incredible!

1-1/2 c. flaked coconut
1/4 c. sugar
2 egg whites

Garnish: 1/4 c. sliced almonds, toasted

Combine coconut, sugar and egg whites in a large bowl; mix well for 2 to 3 minutes. Spray 16 mini muffin cups with non-stick vegetable spray. Press one tablespoonful coconut mixture into bottom and up sides of each cup. Place muffin pan on a baking sheet. Bake at 350 degrees for 13 to 16 minutes, or until tarts begin to turn golden. Let cool for 5 minutes; remove from pan onto wire rack and cool completely. Fill pastry bag fitted with star piping with Chocolate-Cream Filling. Pipe filling evenly into tarts; sprinkle with almonds. Makes 16.

Chocolate-Cream Filling:

1/4 c. butter, softened
1-2/3 c. powdered sugar
2 T. whipping cream
1/4 t. almond extract

1 T. light corn syrup
2 1-oz. sqs. unsweetened chocolate, melted and cooled

Beat butter with an electric mixer at medium speed for one to 2 minutes or until creamy. Continue mixing, gradually adding powdered sugar alternately with cream and extract, for one to 2 minutes or until light and fluffy. Add corn syrup; mix well. Stir in melted chocolate.

Stained Glass Cookies

Linda Harris
Santa Monica, CA

Make lots of fun shapes like stars, hearts, trees...the kids will love helping out.

1/2 c. margarine, softened
1/2 c. shortening
1 c. sugar
1 egg
1 t. vanilla extract

2-1/2 c. all-purpose flour
1/2 t. baking soda
1/2 t. salt
colored hard candies, crushed

Mix margarine and shortening in a bowl. Add sugar, egg and vanilla; set aside. Sift together flour, baking soda and salt; add to margarine mixture and stir well. Form dough into a ball; wrap in wax paper and refrigerate overnight. Shape into long, thin ropes; form ropes into closed shapes such as triangles, circles or stars. Place shapes on greased baking sheets. Fill insides of shapes with crushed candies. Bake at 350 degrees for 8 minutes, or until golden and candy has melted. Makes one to 2 dozen.

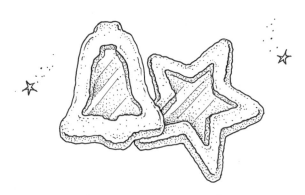

Overlap cookies in a wreath shape and dust with powdered sugar for a snowy look. Perfect for nibbling on before the cookie exchange begins.

Clothespin Cookies

Tina Goodpasture
Meadowview, VA

An old-fashioned treat filled with marshmallow creme.

3 c. all-purpose flour
2 T. sugar
2 c. shortening, divided

2 egg yolks
1 c. water

Combine flour, sugar, one cup shortening, egg yolks and water; blend well. Chill for one hour. Roll out on a floured surface; spread 1/3 cup remaining shortening over surface. Chill for an additional hour. Repeat twice with remaining shortening; chill overnight. Divide dough into 4 parts; roll out 1/4-inch thick on floured surface. Cut into strips 1/2-inch wide by 4 to 5 inches long. Wrap strips tightly around greased wooden clothespins without springs or dowels; place on lightly greased baking sheets. Bake at 400 degrees for 18 to 20 minutes, or until golden. Let cool; remove cookies carefully from clothespins and chill. Using a frosting bag, fill cookies with filling. Makes about 8 dozen.

Filling:

1 c. butter, softened
2 c. powdered sugar

3/4 c. marshmallow creme
1 t. vanilla extract

Mix together butter and powdered sugar with an electric mixer on medium speed until fluffy. Blend in marshmallow creme and extract.

Cover the cookie display table in holiday giftwrap...so whimsical and merry!

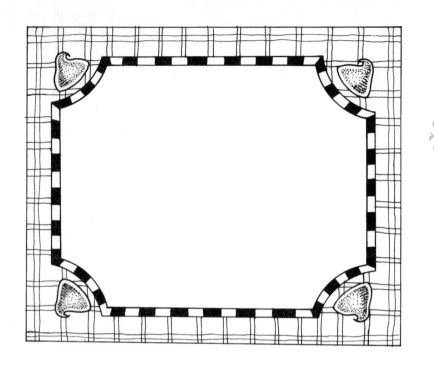

Use our labels for
your goodies!

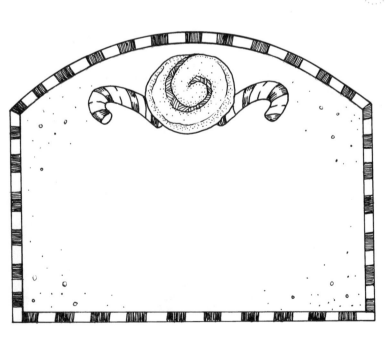

Candy Cane
LANE

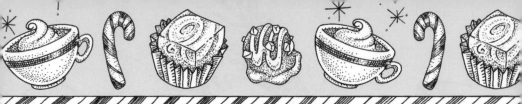

Christmas Snowballs

Jayme Warner
Franklin, IN

*When I take these to a party, I always come home
with an empty tray.*

3-oz. pkg. cream cheese,
   softened
2 t. vanilla or coconut extract
2 c. powdered sugar

2-1/2 c. flaked coconut
Optional: maraschino
   cherries, diced

Blend together cream cheese and extract. Mix in powdered sugar
1/2 cup at a time; add coconut and cherries, if using. Roll into one-inch
balls with greased hands, pressing firmly. Keep refrigerated. Makes 6
to 7 dozen.

Holiday Spiced Tea Mix

Michelle Baltzell
Aberdeen, SD

Warm up with a mug of this after building a snowman!

2 c. sugar
2 c. orange drink mix
3/4 c. instant tea mix

1 T. cinnamon
1 t. ground cloves

Mix all ingredients together. Makes 4-3/4 cups.

Instructions:

Place 2 teaspoons mix in a mug. Add hot water and stir to dissolve.
Makes one serving.

Chocolate-Coconut Bonbons

Melissa Bromen
Marshall, MN

With only 4 ingredients, these are a "must try!"

2 1-oz. sqs. unsweetened
   baking chocolate
14-oz. can sweetened
   condensed milk

2 c. flaked coconut
1/2 c. chopped walnuts

Melt chocolate in the top of a double boiler over boiling water. Remove from heat and stir in remaining ingredients. Drop by teaspoonfuls onto greased baking sheets, shaping with hands into balls. Preheat oven at 350 degrees; turn off heat. Place baking sheets in oven for 20 minutes or until candies have a glazed appearance. Makes 3 dozen.

For mess-less candy making, use a sheet of aluminum foil. Candies such as peanut brittle or fudge can be spread on an aluminum foil-lined baking sheet...no sticking, no clean-up!

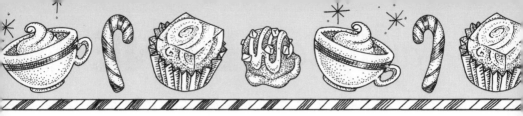

Holiday Wreaths

*Holly Tabler
Mesa, AZ*

*So easy and so fun! While my kids were growing up, they loved
making these festive wreaths. They're adults now, but still
want to make them with their own children.*

30 marshmallows
1/2 c. margarine
1 t. vanilla extract
2 t. green food coloring

3-1/2 c. corn flake cereal
Garnish: red cinnamon
   candies or chopped
   maraschino cherries

Combine marshmallows, margarine and vanilla in a saucepan; melt
slowly over low heat. Stir in food coloring when marshmallows have
melted. Remove from heat; add corn flake cereal and stir until well
coated. Drop by tablespoonfuls onto wax paper; use hands to form into
wreath shapes. Decorate as desired with candies or cherries.
Makes 3 to 4 dozen.

*Serve up cookies on a memory tray...so easy!
Remove the back and glass from a photo frame, lightly
sand the frame with fine-grit sandpaper and coat with
acrylic paint; let dry. Coat with a matte sealer; let dry.
Arrange photos, gift cards, invitations or holiday cards
on the frame backing and replace the glass.*

Angel Candy

Vickie Lowrey
Fallon, NV

Ten years ago, while living in Arkansas, a friend shared this recipe with me. Since then, I've made it every Christmas for family & friends.

24-oz. pkg. white or chocolate melting chocolate, broken
2 c. sweetened corn & oats cereal
2 c. stick pretzels, broken into small pieces
2 c. roasted peanuts or pecans

Place chocolate in a large saucepan over very low heat until melted; stir constantly to prevent burning. Remove from heat; stir in remaining ingredients until well coated. Drop by tablespoonfuls onto wax paper-covered baking sheets. Let cool; store in an airtight container. Makes 3 to 4 dozen.

Arrange candies in a nostalgic glass compote or vintage punch bowl...what a way to display those special sweet treats!

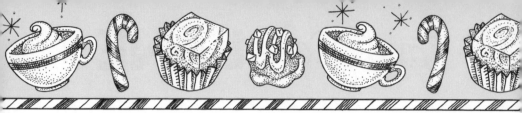

Candy Bar Fudge

Lori Brandes
Wellsville, NY

I hope you enjoy this recipe that I hold dear to my heart.

1/2 c. butter
1/3 c. baking cocoa
1/4 c. brown sugar, packed
1/4 c. milk
3-1/2 c. powdered sugar
1 t. vanilla extract

30 caramels, unwrapped
1 T. water
2 c. salted peanuts
1/2 c. milk chocolate chips
1/2 c. butterscotch chips

Combine butter, cocoa, brown sugar and milk in a microwave-safe bowl. Microwave on high setting until mixture comes to a boil, about 2 minutes. Stir in powdered sugar and vanilla. Pour into a lightly greased 8"x8" baking pan; set aside. In another microwave-safe bowl, combine caramels and water on high setting until melted, about 2 minutes. Stir in peanuts; carefully spread over cocoa layer. Combine milk chocolate and butterscotch chips in a microwave-safe bowl; microwave on high setting until melted, about one minute. Drizzle over caramel layer. Chill until firm; let stand 15 to 20 minutes at room temperature before cutting into squares. Makes one dozen.

What you see before you, my friend,
is the result of a lifetime of chocolate.

-Katharine Hepburn

Holly-Jolly Almond Brittle

Susan White
Lexington, KY

No one can stop munching on this!

1-1/2 c. whole almonds	1 c. sugar
3 T. butter	4 T. water

Spread almonds in a single layer on an ungreased baking sheet. With oven rack at center position, toast at 350 degrees for 10 minutes, stirring occasionally. Melt butter in a small skillet over medium heat. Add toasted almonds and cook, stirring constantly, for about 3 minutes. Set aside. Combine sugar and water in a small saucepan. Bring to a boil, stirring to dissolve sugar. Wash down crystals on sides of pan with a small brush dipped in water; do not stir. Bring to a boil until mixture turns golden. Remove from heat; stir in almonds and butter. Quickly pour onto a greased baking sheet. Let cool; when hardened, break into pieces. Store at room temperature in an airtight container. Makes about one pound.

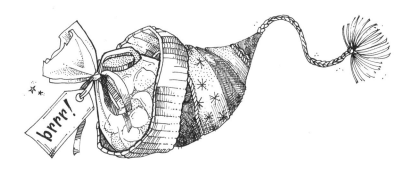

Slip a container of homemade candy inside a woolly toboggan...perfect for a winter swap. A watering can or terra cotta pot become whimsical warm-weather containers.

Candied Nuts

Lois Bohm
Clark, NJ

*A former student gave me the recipe for this delicious treat.
Now I make them every holiday to share.*

1/2 lb. whole nuts, shelled
   and halved
1 egg white
1 t. water

1/2 lb. nuts, finely ground
1/2 c. sugar
1/2 t. cinnamon
1/2 t. salt

Place halved nuts on a lightly greased baking sheet; set aside. Beat
together egg white and water; pour over halved nuts and stir to coat
well. Combine ground nuts, sugar, cinnamon and salt; sprinkle over
coated nuts; mix well. Bake at 200 degrees for one hour, stirring every
15 minutes. Makes about one pound.

Holiday Eggnog

Kim Hacking
Salt Lake City, UT

*For a festive look, hang candy canes along the edges of
the punch bowl.*

1 pt. peppermint ice cream,
   softened
1 qt. eggnog

1 ltr. lemon-lime soda

Mix all ingredients together in a punch bowl; serve immediately.
Makes about 10 cups.

*Give eggnog glasses a sweet touch...dip the rims of
chilled glasses in water, then in sparkly sugar.*

Amish Fudge

Lori Graham
Pittsfield, PA

*Passed down from my mom, this recipe for fudge is
a holiday tradition.*

12-oz. can evaporated milk
4 c. sugar
2 t. vanilla extract
1/2 c. butter
18-oz. jar creamy peanut butter

10-oz. milk chocolate bar,
   chopped
12-oz. pkg. semi-sweet
   chocolate chips
1 c. chopped nuts

Combine evaporated milk and sugar in a large saucepan. Bring to
a boil; lower heat and continue boiling for 10 minutes, stirring
occasionally. Remove from heat; add remaining ingredients except
nuts and mix well. Stir in nuts. Pour into a greased 13"x9" baking pan.
Chill until set; cut into squares. Makes 2-1/2 to 3 dozen.

Buttering the sides of a heavy saucepan
before adding fudge ingredients will help prevent
sugar crystals from forming on the pan.
This will keep fudge creamy, smooth and delicious!

Coconut Thumbprints

Heather Rulli
Gurnee, IL

Coconut lovers will ask for more & more of these sweet treats!

1/2 c. butter, melted
2 c. powdered sugar
3-1/2 c. flaked coconut

1/2 c. semi-sweet chocolate
    chips, melted

Combine butter, sugar and coconut. Stir until well mixed; form into one-inch balls. Place on wax paper-lined baking sheets. Press thumb down on each ball to make a small indentation; spoon a small amount of melted chocolate into each indentation. Refrigerate until chocolate hardens. Store in refrigerator or freezer until serving time. Makes about 1-1/2 to 2-1/2 dozen.

Just for fun, fill ice cream cones with individual candies; wrap each with cellophane and tie off with ribbon. Kids will love 'em!

Candy Cane **LANE**

Creamy Butter Mints

Janice Miller
Huntington, IN

Vary the food coloring depending on the occasion...pastels for springtime or a bridal shower are just perfect.

1-lb. pkg. powdered sugar
1/2 c. butter, softened
2 T. whipping cream

1/4 t. peppermint extract
2 drops red food coloring

Place powdered sugar and butter in a medium bowl. With an electric mixer on medium speed, beat together for 2 to 3 minutes, until creamy. Add cream, extract and food coloring; beat for 3 to 4 minutes until well blended. Shape mixture into 1/2-inch balls; lightly press balls with thumb to form wafers. Place on wire racks and allow to dry overnight, uncovered. Store in an airtight container. Makes 5 dozen.

Instant Peppermint Hot Chocolate

Flo Burtnett
Gage, OK

Sip and relax.

1 T. semi-sweet chocolate chips
1-oz. pkg. hot chocolate mix

3/4 c. boiling water
Garnish: 1 candy cane

Place chips in the bottom of a mug; add hot chocolate mix and water. Stir with a candy cane. Makes one serving.

Merry Minty Chocolates

Nicole Delaura
Cedar City, UT

Everyone will rave over these!

16-oz. pkg. powdered sugar
3 T. butter, softened
2 to 3 t. peppermint extract
1/4 c. evaporated milk

1/2 t. vanilla extract
6-oz. pkg. semi-sweet
   chocolate chips
1 T. shortening

Combine sugar, butter and extract in a bowl; add evaporated milk and mix well. Roll into one-inch balls; place on wax paper-lined baking sheets. Chill for 20 minutes. Flatten balls to 1/4-inch thick with the bottom of a glass tumbler; chill for an additional 30 minutes. Melt together chocolate chips and shortening in a saucepan over low heat. Use a toothpick or candy dipper to dip patties into melted chocolate; return to wax paper and chill. Makes about 5 dozen.

Candies are easy to tote along...before placing in a carrier, layer candy between colorful sheets of vellum to keep them from sticking together.

Stir & Spoon Fudge Drops

Mary Jo Babiarz
Spring Grove, IL

So easy to make, I like to whip up a batch for gifts.

2 T. butter
1-2/3 c. sugar
2/3 c. evaporated milk
1/4 t. salt
1 t. vanilla extract
2 c. mini marshmallows

1-1/2 c. semi-sweet
   chocolate chips
1/2 c. nuts, coarsely chopped
1/2 c. raisins
1/2 c. dried apricots,
   finely chopped

Combine butter, sugar, evaporated milk and salt in a saucepan over medium heat. Bring to a boil; when mixture begins to bubble around the edges, lower heat and cook for 4 to 5 minutes. Remove from heat and add remaining ingredients. Stir vigorously for one minute, until marshmallows melt and mixture is blended. Drop by teaspoonfuls onto wax paper; let cool. Makes about 2 pounds.

Pack candies into a basket or handy tote the cookie exchange hostess can keep long after the swap is over. What a thoughtful thank-you gift!

Peanut Butter Fudge

Flo Snodderly
North Vernon, IN

Creamy and smooth...this will disappear quickly.

2 c. sugar
1/2 c. milk

7-oz. jar marshmallow creme
1-1/3 c. creamy peanut butter

Bring sugar and milk to a boil in a saucepan; boil for 3 minutes.
Remove from heat. Add marshmallow creme and peanut butter;
mix well. Quickly pour into a greased 8"x8" baking pan. Chill until
set; cut into squares. Makes one dozen.

Chocolate Variation:

To make chocolate fudge, use 2 cups semi-sweet chocolate chips
instead of the peanut butter chips and the peanut butter.

Mocha Punch

Yvonne Hatfield
Norman, OK

This is a great, flavorful make-ahead punch.

1-1/2 qts. water
1/2 c. chocolate
   drink mix
1/2 c. sugar

1/4 c. instant coffee granules
1/2 gal. vanilla ice cream
1/2 gal. chocolate ice cream
Garnish: whipped cream

Bring water to a boil; remove from heat. Add drink mix, sugar and
coffee granules; stir until dissolved. Pour into a container; cover.
Refrigerate for at least 4 hours. Remove from refrigerator at least
30 minutes before serving; pour into a punch bowl. Spoon in ice
cream; stir until partially melted. Garnish with whipped cream.
Serves about 20 to 25.

Easy Microwave Butter Toffee

Sherri Fisher
Wichita, KS

I love to wrap this toffee up in decorative tins to share with friends and neighbors. It's so quick & easy!

1-1/3 c. sugar
1 c. butter, softened
2 T. water
1 T. dark corn syrup
1 t. vanilla extract
3/4 c. semi-sweet
   chocolate chips
2/3 c. chopped walnuts

Combine sugar, butter, water and corn syrup in a large microwave-safe bowl. Microwave on high setting for 4 minutes; stir. Heat an additional 6 to 8 minutes, stirring every 2 minutes, until thickened and golden. Add vanilla; stir well. Pour into a 13"x9" baking pan lined with ungreased aluminum foil. Spread chocolate chips over top; sprinkle with walnuts. Let cool completely; break into pieces. Makes about one pound.

A retro tea towel is a quick & easy wrap-up for candies. Place candy in the middle of a towel and bring the corners together. Secure with a length of wax twine and you're done!

Cinnamon Rock Candy

Sharon Jones
Oklahoma City, OK

You can substitute green coloring and spearmint oil for a minty variation of this candy.

1 c. water
3-3/4 c. sugar
1-1/4 c. light corn syrup

1 t. red food coloring
1 to 2 t. cinnamon oil
1/3 c. powdered sugar

In a large heavy saucepan, combine water, sugar, corn syrup and food coloring. Bring to a boil over medium heat, stirring occasionally. Cover and heat for 3 minutes; uncover. Cook without stirring on medium-high heat until mixture reaches the hard-crack stage, or 290 to 300 degrees on a candy thermometer, about 25 minutes. Remove from heat; stir in cinnamon oil. Immediately pour onto a greased jelly-roll pan. Let cool completely, about 45 minutes. Break into pieces using the edge of a metal mallet. Sprinkle both sides with powdered sugar. Store in an airtight container. Makes 2 pounds.

All wrapped up! A pretty ruby red glass bowl filled with candy then wrapped in clear cellophane is a very merry way to tote candy to any get-together. Top it off with a festive printed ribbon.

Candy Cane LANE

Strawberry Fudge Balls

Dana Cunningham
Lafayette, LA

Made with strawberry preserves, this can be enjoyed year 'round!

8-oz. pkg. cream cheese,
  softened
6-oz. pkg. semi-sweet chocolate
  chips, melted

3/4 c. vanilla wafer crumbs
1/4 c. strawberry preserves
1/2 c. toasted almonds,
  finely chopped

Beat cream cheese with an electric mixer at medium speed until
creamy. Add melted chocolate; blend until smooth. Stir in crumbs and
preserves; cover and chill for one hour. Shape into one-inch balls. Roll
in chopped nuts; chill. Makes 4 dozen.

Raspberry Limeade

Sharon Tillman
Hampton, VA

Substitute a 10-ounce package of frozen raspberries if you'd like.

3 c. raspberries
7 c. water, divided

1 c. sugar
1 c. lime juice

Purée berries with one cup water; strain through a fine sieve and set
aside. Combine sugar with one cup water in a small saucepan; bring
to a boil. Simmer until reduced to one cup, about 15 minutes. Let cool.
Combine raspberry mixture in a pitcher with sugar mixture, lime juice
and remaining 5 cups water. Mix well and chill. Serve in tall glasses
over ice. Serves 5 to 7.

*Give a punch bowl a festive feel by hanging
candy canes around the edge!*

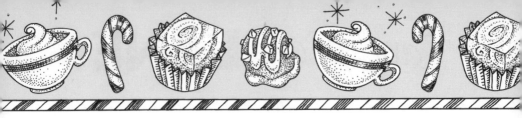

Peanut Butter-Cocoa Truffles

Marian Buckley
Fontana, CA

Let the kids help roll these in all the yummy garnishes!

3/4 c. butter
1 c. peanut butter chips
1/2 c. baking cocoa
14-oz. can sweetened
    condensed milk

1 T. vanilla extract
Garnish: baking cocoa, finely
    chopped nuts, graham
    cracker crumbs

Melt butter and peanut butter chips in a large saucepan over low heat,
stirring often. Add cocoa; stir until smooth. Stir in condensed milk.
Stir constantly until mixture is thick and glossy, about 4 minutes.
Remove from heat; stir in vanilla. Chill for 2 hours or until firm enough
to handle. Shape into one-inch balls; roll in cocoa, nuts or crumbs.
Chill until firm, about one hour. Store covered in refrigerator.
Makes about 3-1/2 dozen.

Stack candies in an old-fashioned apothecary
jar...they stay fresh and it's a snap to twist off the lid
when it's time for swapping!

Chocolate Truffles

Margaret Hanson-Maddox
Montpelier, IN

Keep plenty on hand for drop-in guests or wrap up several for the newspaper and letter carriers.

8 1-oz. sqs. unsweetened
   baking chocolate
1/3 c. plus 2 T. half-and-half,
   divided
1/3 c. butter-flavored shortening
3 egg yolks
1/3 c. powdered sugar
2/3 c. finely chopped pecans

In a medium saucepan, melt chocolate over low heat, stirring continuously. Gradually stir 1/3 cup half-and-half into melted chocolate until smooth. Add shortening; stir until melted and remove from heat. Stir one tablespoon chocolate mixture into egg yolks; add yolks, powdered sugar and remaining half-and-half to saucepan. Beat with an electric mixer at high speed until well blended. Refrigerate for 2 hours or until firm. Shape into one-inch balls; roll in nuts. Refrigerate until serving time. Makes 2 to 2-1/2 dozen.

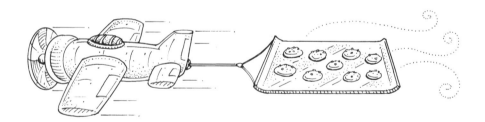

For candy making at high altitudes, keep in mind that for every 500 feet above sea level, you'll need to decrease the temperature by one degree. For example, if you live at 3500 feet, and the recipe calls for cooking candy to 234 degrees, simply cook it to 227 degrees.

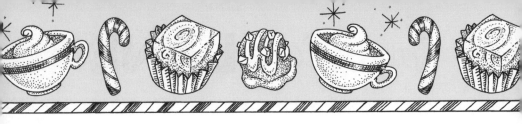

Walnut-Cherry Fudge

SueMary Burford-Smith
Tulsa, OK

Get a jump on holiday baking...this freezes well for up to 3 months.

2 c. sugar
1/3 c. sour cream
1/3 c. light corn syrup
3 T. butter

1/4 t. salt
2 t. vanilla extract
1/4 c. dried cherries
1 c. walnuts, coarsely chopped

Combine sugar, sour cream, corn syrup, butter and salt in a saucepan. Bring to a boil; cook and stir until mixture reaches the soft-ball stage, or 234 to 243 degrees on a candy thermometer. Remove from heat; let cool for 10 minutes. Beat mixture with an electric mixer on medium speed for 8 minutes, until white and fluffy. Immediately stir in vanilla, cherries and nuts; pour into a greased 9"x9" baking pan. Let stand until firm; cut into 2-inch squares. Store in an airtight container. Makes about 1-1/2 dozen.

Before making candy, check the weather. On rainy or humid days, the cooking time can increase or the candy may not set up at all. This is because sugar attracts water, so wait for a clear, crisp day to enjoy candy making!

4-Chip Fudge

Renae Scheiderer
Beallsville, OH

Very rich!

3/4 c. butter
3 T. milk
14-oz. can sweetened
   condensed milk
12-oz. pkg. semi-sweet
   chocolate chips
12-oz. pkg. milk chocolate chips

10-oz. pkg. peanut butter chips
1 c. butterscotch chips
7-oz. jar marshmallow creme
1/2 t. vanilla extract
1/2 t. almond extract
1 c. chopped walnuts

In a large saucepan, melt butter over low heat. Add milk, condensed milk, chocolate chips and peanut butter chips. Remove from heat; stir in butterscotch chips, marshmallow creme and extracts until well blended. Stir in nuts. Spread in an aluminum foil-lined, greased 13"x9" baking pan. Refrigerate until set. Lift out of pan; remove aluminum foil and cut into squares. Store in refrigerator. Makes 4-1/2 pounds.

Line a new terra cotta pot with wax paper and fill with candy. Place an inverted saucer on top as a lid and keep them secure with a length of raffia or jute...what could be easier?

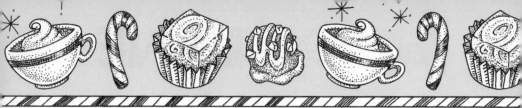

Nana's Christmas Caramels

Judi Towner
Towanda, PA

*There was a special time of excitement and anticipation in our house
back in the 1950's when our grandmother made Christmas candy.
It would be a cold, snowy day and my brothers and I were thrilled
with these yummy caramels. We could always count on getting
them in our Christmas stockings!*

1 c. butter	1 c. brown sugar, packed
1 c. milk	1 c. light corn syrup
1 c. whipping cream	1 t. vanilla extract
2 c. sugar	

Grease around the top of a Dutch oven to prevent boiling over. Melt
butter in Dutch oven; use a brush and some of the butter to grease an
aluminum foil-lined 9"x9" baking pan. Set pan aside. Add remaining
ingredients except vanilla to the Dutch oven. Over medium-high heat,
cook and stir until mixture reaches the soft-ball stage, or 234 to
243 degrees on a candy thermometer, about 35 minutes. Remove from
heat; stir in vanilla and quickly pour caramel into prepared pan. Let
stand at room temperature or in the refrigerator until firm. Grasp ends
of aluminum foil; lift out caramel and invert onto a cutting board.
Cut into 1"x1" squares; wrap each in a square of wax paper and twist
ends. Makes 7 dozen.

*Keep it fun...serve up glasses of frosty punch
on a tray covered with freshly fallen snow!*

178

Candy Cane **LANE**

Chocolate-Covered Cherry Bites

Kristie Rigo
Friedens, PA

I think these taste better than a chocolate-covered cherry...definitely addictive!

2 16-oz. pkgs. powdered sugar
14-oz. pkg. flaked coconut
16-oz. jar maraschino cherries,
   drained and chopped
1/2 c. chopped pecans

14-oz. can sweetened
   condensed milk
16-oz. pkg. melting chocolate,
   chopped

Combine powdered sugar, coconut, cherries and pecans in a large bowl; mix well. Top with condensed milk; mix well with hands until thoroughly combined and sugar is dissolved. Roll into one-inch balls; place on wax paper-lined baking sheets. Refrigerate overnight. Place chocolate in a microwave-safe container; heat on high setting until melted, stirring after every minute. Using a toothpick or candy dipper, dip chilled cherry balls into melted chocolate. Return to wax paper-lined baking sheets; refrigerate until set. Makes about 4 dozen.

Make a splash!
Fill a brand-new, small,
fish bowl with candy.

Chocolate Popcorn Crunch

Jessica Parker
Mulvane, KS

Makes a bunch...ideal for gatherings any time of year!

14 c. popped popcorn
3 c. crispy rice cereal
2 c. dry-roasted peanuts

1-1/2 lbs. melting chocolate,
   chopped
3 T. creamy peanut butter

Combine popcorn, cereal and peanuts in a very large bowl; mix well and set aside. In a large microwave-safe bowl, combine chocolate and peanut butter. Microwave for 2 to 3 minutes on high setting or until melted, stirring after every minute. Pour over popcorn mixture, tossing to coat well. Spread onto baking sheets sprayed with non-stick vegetable spray; let cool thoroughly. Break apart; store up to 5 days in an airtight container. Makes 28 to 30 servings.

Frosty Orange Slush

Tori Willis
Champaign, IL

Frothy and so yummy!

6-oz. can frozen orange
   juice concentrate
1 c. water
1 c. milk

1/2 c. sugar
1 t. vanilla extract
8 to 10 ice cubes

Combine all ingredients in a blender. Process until thick and slushy. Makes 4 cups.

Fabulous Festive Candy

Jennie Wiseman
Coshocton, OH

So simple to make and everyone will be asking for more.

10-oz. pkg. mini pretzels
5 c. doughnut-shaped oat cereal
5 c. bite-size crispy corn
   cereal squares
2 c. salted peanuts

16-oz. pkg. candy-coated
   chocolates
2 12-oz. pkgs. white
   chocolate chips
3 T. oil

Combine pretzels, cereals, peanuts and candy-coated chocolates in a large bowl; mix well and set aside. Place chocolate chips and oil in a microwave-safe bowl; heat on high setting for 2 minutes, stirring once. Microwave on high setting for an additional 10 seconds; stir until smooth. Pour over mixture in bowl; mix well. Spread onto wax paper-lined baking sheets. Let cool; break apart. Store in an airtight container. Makes 5 quarts.

Old-fashioned milk bottles are just right for holding candy mixes.

Grandma Rowland's Fondant

Cindy Neel
Gooseberry Patch

The holidays wouldn't be complete without several batches of Grandma's Fondant. Making this candy gives me great thoughts of childhood Christmases and a kinship with generations past.

1/4 t. peppermint oil
1 drop red or green food coloring
2 c. sugar
1-1/4 c. water

2 T. light corn syrup
1/4 t. salt
Garnish: walnut halves

Place peppermint oil and food coloring on a large buttered platter; set aside. Combine sugar, water, corn syrup and salt in a saucepan; bring to a boil. Heat until mixture reaches the soft-ball stage, or 234 to 243 degrees on a candy thermometer. Slowly pour over prepared platter. Work mixture with a knife, pushing it from side to side until cool enough to touch. Knead with hands until smooth. Roll into one-inch balls; press a walnut half on top of each. Arrange on wax paper to set; store in airtight container with wax paper between layers. Makes 1-1/2 to 2 dozen.

Turn this year's cookie swap into a sledding party! Afterward, friends can warm up with hot cocoa and fireside sweets until their mittens and socks are dry.

Church Windows

Kelly Goralski
Lapeer, MI

Thick, coconut covered slices of chocolatey marshmallows.

12-oz. pkg. semi-sweet
  chocolate chips
1/2 c. margarine
10-oz. pkg. colored mini
  marshmallows

1 c. chopped walnuts
7-oz. pkg. flaked coconut

Melt together chocolate chips and margarine in a saucepan over very low heat until smooth, stirring often. Pour over marshmallows and nuts in a mixing bowl. Shape into a 12"x4" roll; roll in coconut. Let cool; slice into 3/4-inch thick slices. Store in refrigerator. Makes about 4 dozen.

Gather up those mismatched teacups,
set a tea light inside and line them up along the mantel
for a beautiful holiday glow. So warm and
inviting when friends are visiting.

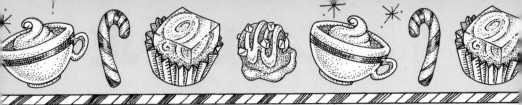

Marshmallow Puffs

Lisa Langston
Conroe, TX

My daughter's favorite candy recipe...we're sure you'll love it too!

36 marshmallows
1-1/2 c. semi-sweet
   chocolate chips

1/2 c. creamy peanut butter
2 T. butter

Arrange marshmallows in an aluminum foil-lined, greased
9"x9" baking pan; set aside. Combine chocolate chips, peanut butter
and butter in a microwave-safe container. Heat on high setting,
stirring after each 30 seconds, until melted. Stir until smooth; pour
over marshmallows in pan. Chill completely; cut into squares between
marshmallows. Makes 3 dozen.

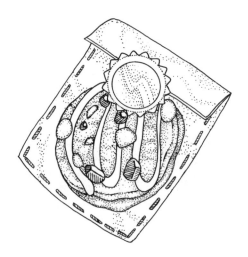

*It's easy to wrap up slightly sticky candies
to take to a cookie exchange. Use red thread to stitch
together two rectangles of wax paper that's cut slightly
larger than the candy. Leave one side open, slip the
candy inside and seal with a sticker.*

Candy Cane **LANE**

Aunt Mary's Praline Pecans

Sandy White
Elmer, LA

Made in the microwave, what could be easier?

2 c. sugar
1 c. brown sugar, packed
1 c. evaporated milk
2 c. chopped pecans

2 T. margarine
1 t. vanilla extract
1/8 t. salt

Combine sugars and evaporated milk in a microwave-safe container. Microwave on high setting for 6 minutes; stir well. Add nuts, margarine, vanilla and salt; heat on high setting for an additional 6 minutes. Stir until thick; drop by teaspoonfuls onto wax paper. Let cool. Makes about 3 dozen.

White Christmas Punch

Linda Hartsfield
Jonesboro, LA

You can divide the recipe in half for smaller get-togethers.

2 c. sugar
1 c. water
12-oz. can evaporated milk

1 T. almond extract
6 2-ltr. bottles lemon-lime soda
3 1/2 gals. vanilla ice cream

Combine sugar and water in a saucepan; heat until sugar dissolves. Remove from heat; add milk and almond extract. Cool; chill until ready to serve. Transfer to a punch bowl; add soda. Top with spoonfuls of ice cream. Makes about 3-1/4 gallons.

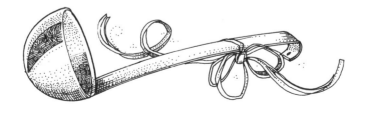

Caramel-Chocolate Pretzel Rods

Michele Carathers
Dalton, OH

Line an empty coffee can or a new, unused paint can with colorful plastic wrap or wax paper, then fill with these treats. My co-workers loved them...you will too!

14-oz. pkg. caramels,
  unwrapped
1/3 c. evaporated milk
10-oz. pkg. pretzel rods

16-oz. pkg. semi-sweet
  chocolate chips
Optional: 8-oz. pkg.
  chopped pecans

In a medium saucepan, combine caramels and evaporated milk. Cook over medium heat until caramels are melted, stirring constantly. Spoon caramel over pretzel rods, one at a time, leaving about one inch uncovered. Lay pretzels on a wax paper-covered baking sheet until slightly hardened. Melt chocolate in a second saucepan over medium heat, stirring constantly. Carefully pick up caramel-coated pretzels, one at a time, and spoon melted chocolate over them, leaving a small amount of caramel uncoated. Return pretzels to wax paper-covered baking sheet; sprinkle with pecans, if desired. Let cool completely. Store in a covered container. Makes about 3/4 pound.

Tie on a pretty cookie name tag so everyone knows just what treat you've brought to share. To dress up a plain tag, give it a retro look with a trim of old-fashioned tinsel.

Candy Cane LANE

Peanut Clusters

Toni Smith
Folsom, CA

A classic everyone expects around the holidays...so yummy!

16-oz. pkg. dark melting
   chocolate, chopped
1/4 c. creamy peanut butter

1 c. semi-sweet chocolate chips
1 c. salted peanuts
1-1/2 c. mini marshmallows

Melt chocolate in a microwave-safe container for 2 minutes on high setting, until soft. Add peanut butter; microwave for one minute and stir together. Add chocolate chips; stir until melted. Add peanuts and marshmallows; stir until completely coated. Drop by teaspoonfuls on wax paper; let cool. Makes 5-1/2 to 6 dozen.

Vintage postcards make a simple but oh-so-pretty table centerpiece. Coil strands of silver-colored wire and insert them into vintage salt & pepper shaker holes for instant card holders!

From the
Kitchen
of:

To:

Let us eat
Cookies!

From:

*Just copy, color
and go!*

COOKIE
TIME!

To:

From:

Very Merry
MIXES

Peanutty Cookie Mix in a Jar

Christina Kostohryz
Wooster, OH

For some added whimsy, I like to wrap a length of
beaded wire around the jar before giving.

3/4 c. salted peanuts
3/4 c. brown sugar, packed
3/4 c. sugar
3/4 c. peanut butter chips

1-1/2 c. all-purpose flour
1 t. baking soda
1/4 t. salt

Layer ingredients in a one-quart, wide-mouth canning jar. Press each layer firmly in place before adding the next ingredient. Seal lid tightly. Attach instructions.

Instructions:

Empty jar of cookie mix into a large mixing bowl; mix well. Add 1/2 cup softened butter, 1/2 cup creamy peanut butter, one beaten egg and one teaspoon vanilla extract. Mix until completely blended. Shape into walnut-size balls; arrange 2 inches apart on greased baking sheets. Bake at 350 degrees for 12 to 14 minutes or until edges are golden. Cool for 5 minutes on baking sheets. Remove cookies to wire rack to cool completely. Makes 3 dozen.

When making layered jar mixes, be sure to pack the layers together firmly. Use a tamper or even a small juice glass to tightly pack down the ingredients so everything fits just right.

Cappuccino Mix in a Jar

*Janeen Polen
Spangdahlem AFB, Germany*

*How clever! Spoon this mix into a plastic zipping bag, then tuck it
into a speckled enamelware coffee pot.*

1 c. powdered non-dairy creamer
1 c. chocolate drink mix
3/4 c. instant coffee granules
1/2 c. sugar
1/2 t. cinnamon
1/4 t. nutmeg

Combine all ingredients in a mixing bowl; place in an airtight
container. Attach instructions. Makes 4 cups.

Instructions:

Place 2 tablespoons mix in a mug; add 3/4 cup boiling water.
Stir until dissolved. Makes one serving.

Tie a vintage silver spoon onto a jar of
Cappuccino Mix...it adds a special touch!

Pfeffernuesse Cookie Mix in a Jar

Carol Lytle
Columbus, OH

Traditionally, these firm cookies were meant to be dunked and enjoyed during long visits and get-togethers. So why not make a batch ahead of time, brew a pot of tea and invite friends over to catch up? They can take the jar mix home as a reminder of a fun afternoon together.

4 c. all-purpose flour
1-1/4 t. baking soda
1/2 c. sugar
1/2 t. nutmeg

1-1/2 t. cinnamon
1/2 t. ground cloves
1/8 t. pepper

Combine all ingredients in a mixing bowl; mix well. Place in a one-quart, wide-mouth canning jar; press to pack and seal tightly. Attach instructions.

Instructions:

Combine 3/4 cup light molasses and 1/2 cup softened butter in a large saucepan. Heat and stir until butter melts; cool to room temperature. Stir in 2 eggs and cookie mix; mix well, cover and chill several hours or overnight. Shape dough into walnut-size balls. Arrange 2 inches apart on greased cookie sheets; bake at 350 degrees for 12 to 14 minutes. Cool on wire racks; roll in 1/3 cup powdered sugar. Makes 5 dozen.

Wrap jar mixes with clever seasonal toppers...in fall, place a golden leaf over the lid and secure with kitchen string or jute. In summer, make it a bright green leaf! In spring a dainty handkerchief makes a pretty topper, while a glittery paper snowflake is perfect for winter.

Cowboy Cookie Mix in a Jar

Samantha Starks
Madison, WI

These oversized cookies are a blend of favorite trail mix ingredients with a classic oatmeal cookie.

1-1/3 c. quick-cooking oats, uncooked
1/2 c. brown sugar, packed
1/2 c. sugar
1/2 c. chopped pecans

1 c. semi-sweet chocolate chips
1-1/3 c. all-purpose flour
1 t. baking powder
1 t. baking soda
1/4 t. salt

Layer ingredients in a one-quart, wide-mouth canning jar in the order given, pressing after each layer to pack. Seal tightly. Attach instructions.

Instructions:

Combine 1/2 cup softened butter, one egg, one teaspoon vanilla extract and cookie mix in a large bowl; mix well. Shape into walnut-size balls and arrange 2 inches apart on greased baking sheets. Bake at 350 degrees for 11 to 13 minutes; cool on wire racks. Makes 3 dozen.

Top a jar of Cowboy Cookie Mix with a pint-size cowboy hat or wrap a bandanna around the middle...tie it all up with a jute "lasso!"

Chocolate Candy Cookie Mix in a Jar

Lynn Williams
Muncie, IN

*For a quick & easy teacher gift, I like to set this jar mix inside a
gingham-lined wire basket. Toss in a couple of apples, just for fun!*

3/4 c. brown sugar, packed
1/4 c. sugar
1-1/2 c. mini candy-coated
   chocolates

2 c. all-purpose flour
1/2 t. baking soda
1/4 t. salt

Layer brown sugar, sugar and candy-coated chocolates in a one-quart,
wide-mouth canning jar, pressing after each layer to pack; set aside.
Combine flour, baking soda and salt in a mixing bowl; mix well and
add to jar, pressing to pack. Seal tightly. Attach instructions.

Instructions:

Empty cookie mix into a large bowl; mix well. Add 3/4 cup softened
butter; mix until the dough resembles coarse crumbs. Set aside. In a
small bowl, beat together one egg with one teaspoon vanilla extract;
stir into the flour mixture until well combined. Shape into walnut-size
balls; arrange 2 inches apart on parchment paper-lined baking sheets.
Bake at 350 degrees for 10 to 14 minutes, until edges are golden; cool
on wire racks. Makes 2 dozen.

*Layered mixes are terrific for college students. Fill
a care package with mixes, a phone card, pre-stamped
envelopes, family photos, favorite snacks and quarters
for laundry day...especially perfect at exam time!*

Café Au Lait Mix

Mary Murray
Mount Vernon, OH

I doubled this recipe and spooned it into a vintage-style cream pitcher. It was fun for friends to sample as they enjoyed dessert and coffee.

2 c. powdered milk
1/2 c. instant coffee granules
1/2 c. powdered sugar

1/2 t. cinnamon
1/2 t. ground cloves
1/2 t. allspice

Combine all ingredients until well blended; pour into an airtight container and attach instructions. Makes about 3 cups.

Instructions:

Place 1/4 cup mix in a mug; add 2/3 cup boiling water. Stir to blend. Top with whipped cream, if desired. Makes one serving.

Fill a vintage thermos with a dry cocoa, coffee or cider mix...what clever gift packaging!

Snowball Cookie Mix in a Jar

Anna McMaster
Portland, OR

Deliver jars to friends in the neighborhood while caroling...
sure to bring smiles!

1/2 c. powdered sugar
2 c. all-purpose flour

1 c. chopped pecans

Combine sugar and flour; pour into a one-quart, wide-mouth canning jar. Top with pecans; seal tightly. Attach instructions.

Instructions:

Blend together 3/4 cup shortening and 1/4 cup softened margarine in a medium bowl. Stir in 2 teaspoons vanilla extract; add contents of jar and mix well. Roll dough into one-inch balls and arrange on greased baking sheets. Bake at 325 degrees for 20 to 25 minutes until golden. Let cool; roll in powdered sugar. Makes 4 dozen.

A woolly scarf wrapped around a jar of Snowball Cookie Mix will be a welcome surprise for any mom who's home with kids on a "school's closed" snow day!

Gumdrop Cookie Mix in a Jar

Rhonda Reeder
Ellicott City, MD

Kids seem to love making these mixes...of course,
there's lots of candy nibbling too!

1-3/4 c. all-purpose flour	1/2 c. brown sugar, packed
1 t. baking powder	3/4 c. sugar
1/2 t. baking soda	1-1/2 c. gumdrops, chopped

Combine flour, baking powder and baking soda; place in a one-quart, wide-mouth canning jar. Top with brown sugar, pressing to pack. Toss sugar with gumdrops to coat; add to jar. Seal jar tightly. Attach instructions.

Instructions:

Remove gumdrops from jar and set aside. Empty remaining mix into a large mixing bowl; stir to combine. Add 1/2 cup softened butter, one beaten egg and one teaspoon vanilla extract. Mix until completely blended. Fold in gumdrops; shape into walnut-size balls and arrange 2 inches apart on greased baking sheets. Bake at 375 degrees for 12 to 14 minutes until edges are golden. Cool 5 minutes on baking sheets; remove to wire racks to cool completely. Makes 2-1/2 dozen.

Tie a strand of jingle bells around a jar mix...their cheery music just gets everyone in the holiday mood!

Amaretto Cocoa Mix

Melody Taynor
Everett, WA

This is a welcome gift to keep on hand for surprise visits during the busy holiday season! Just pile in a basket and set by the door.

10-1/2 c. powdered milk
4 c. powdered sugar
2 8-oz. jars amaretto-flavored
    powdered non-dairy creamer

3-1/2 c. baking cocoa
1/2 t. salt

Combine all ingredients together; mix well. Pour equally into eight, one-pint canning jars; seal tightly and attach instructions.
Makes 8 jars.

Instructions:

Place 3 heaping tablespoonfuls mix in a mug. Fill with hot water or milk; stir to dissolve. Makes one serving.

Don't forget to give a bag of marshmallows
with a cocoa mix...perfect pairing!

Toffee Cookie Mix in a Jar

Laura Jones
Louisville, KY

Bet you can't eat just one of these crunchy cookies!

2/3 c. toffee chips
1/2 c. chopped pecans
1/2 c. dark brown sugar, packed

2 c. buttermilk biscuit baking
  mix, divided
1/2 c. light brown sugar, packed

Layer toffee chips, pecans, dark brown sugar, one cup biscuit baking mix, light brown sugar and remaining baking mix in a one-quart, wide-mouth canning jar, pressing lightly after each layer to pack. Fill any additional space at the top of the jar with additional toffee chips and pecans. Seal tightly. Attach instructions.

Instructions:

Empty cookie mix into a medium bowl. Stir in 1/2 cup softened butter, one beaten egg and one teaspoon vanilla extract; mix well. Shape into one-inch balls; arrange on greased baking sheets. Bake at 375 degrees for 10 to 12 minutes or until cookies are golden. Makes 2-1/2 dozen.

Tuck a jar mix into a warm & cozy polar fleece cap for gift giving. Make it a warm-weather gift by setting it inside a child's sand pail!

White Christmas Mix in a Jar

Zoe Bennett
Columbia, SC

*These easy-to-make cookies are sweet for any holiday occasion.
Top the jar with a jingle bell wreath.*

1/2 c. macadamia nuts, chopped
1/2 c. white melting
   chocolate, chopped
1/2 c. dark brown sugar, packed

2 c. buttermilk biscuit
   baking mix, divided
1/2 c. light brown sugar, packed

Layer nuts, chocolate, dark brown sugar, one cup biscuit baking mix, light brown sugar and remaining baking mix in a one-quart, wide-mouth canning jar, pressing lightly after each layer to pack. Seal tightly. Attach instructions.

Instructions:

Empty cookie mix into a medium bowl. Stir in 1/2 cup softened butter, one beaten egg and one teaspoon vanilla extract; mix well. Shape into one-inch balls; arrange on greased baking sheets. Bake at 375 degrees for 10 to 12 minutes or until cookies are golden. Makes 2-1/2 dozen.

Gather together your girlfriends and create layered jar mixes assembly-line style! It's such fun to chat and catch up and before you know it, you've created mixes galore!

Bavarian Mint Coffee Mix

Sherry Gordon
Arlington Heights, IL

A cozy gift to chase away winter's chill!

1/4 c. powdered
   non-dairy creamer
1/3 c. powdered sugar

1/4 c. instant coffee granules
2 T. baking cocoa
3 peppermint hard candies

Combine all ingredients in a blender or food processor. Blend until candies are finely ground. Pour into a one-quart, wide-mouth canning jar; seal tightly and decorate as desired. Attach instructions. Makes about one cup.

Instructions:

Pour 2 to 3 rounded tablespoonfuls of mix into a mug. Add boiling water and stir to dissolve. Makes one serving.

Slip a mitten over the top of a jar of Bavarian Mint Coffee Mix and then slip the instructions inside the matching mitten for a charming little gift.

Trail Mix Cookie Mix in a Jar

Nancy Wise
Little Rock, AR

This is a cookie everyone will enjoy. Give with an old-fashioned bottle of icy cold milk.

1/2 c. brown sugar, packed
1/2 c. sugar
3/4 c. wheat germ
1/3 c. quick-cooking oats,
   uncooked

1 c. raisins
1/3 c. flaked coconut
1/2 c. all-purpose flour
1 t. baking powder

Layer brown sugar, sugar, wheat germ, oats, raisins and coconut in a one-quart wide-mouth canning jar, pressing gently after each layer to pack. Set aside. Combine flour and baking powder; layer over coconut, pressing to pack. Seal tightly. Attach instructions.

Instructions:

Empty cookie mix into a large mixing bowl; mix thoroughly. Add 1/2 cup softened butter, one beaten egg and one teaspoon vanilla extract; mix until completely blended. Shape into walnut-size balls; arrange 2 inches apart on greased baking sheets. Bake at 350 degrees for 12 to 14 minutes until edges are golden. Cool for 5 minutes on baking sheets; remove to wire racks to cool completely. Makes 2-1/2 dozen.

Kids will love a dunking kit: a yummy cookie mix, carton of milk and big mugs...everything a serious cookie dunker needs!

Potato Chip Cookie Mix in a Jar

Dale Duncan
Waterloo, LA

No one can guess the secret ingredient!

2-1/2 c. all-purpose flour
1 t. baking powder
1 c. sugar

1-1/2 c. potato chips, crushed
2/3 c. pecans, chopped

Combine flour and baking powder in a small bowl; mix well and set aside. Layer sugar, chips, pecans and flour mixture in a one-quart wide-mouth canning jar, pressing after each layer to pack. Seal tightly and decorate jar as desired. Attach instructions.

Instructions:

Empty cookie mix into a large mixing bowl; stir to combine thoroughly. Add one cup softened butter and one teaspoon vanilla; mix until well blended. Shape into walnut-size balls; flatten and arrange on ungreased baking sheets. Bake at 350 degrees for 14 to 18 minutes until golden. Let cool 5 minutes on baking sheets; remove to wire racks to cool completely. Makes 2-1/2 dozen.

It's a snap to personalize a gift tag with buttons... just glue a variety of same-color buttons in the shape of a friend's initial.

Cozy Homemade Hot Cocoa Mix

Penny McShane
Lombard, IL

Snowy giftwrap that couldn't be easier. Set a jar of cocoa mix in the middle of a length of wax paper, then gather paper at the top of the jar. Tie with glittery ribbon.

8 1-qt. pkgs. powdered milk
16-oz. pkg. powdered sugar
16-oz. can chocolate drink mix

8-oz. jar powdered
non-dairy creamer

Combine all ingredients in a large mixing bowl; mix well with a whisk. Store in airtight containers. Attach instructions. Makes 15 cups.

Instructions:

Pour 4 heaping teaspoonfuls of mix into a mug; add boiling water and stir to dissolve. Makes one serving.

Invite friends for a cookie swap using festive ornaments for invitations. Use a paint pen to include all the important information...date, time and location and hand deliver to see the smiles!

Oatmeal-Raisin Cookie Mix in a Jar

Judy Adams
Wooster, OH

This is a year 'round favorite at our house. We like to make several jars and keep them on the pantry shelf.

1/3 c. raisins
1/3 c. chopped walnuts
1/2 c. dark brown sugar, packed
1 c. quick-cooking oats,
   uncooked

2 c. buttermilk biscuit baking
   mix, divided
1/2 c. light brown sugar, packed

Layer raisins, walnuts, dark brown sugar, oats, one cup biscuit baking mix, light brown sugar and remaining baking mix in a one-quart, wide-mouth canning jar, pressing lightly after each layer to pack. Fill any additional space at the top of the jar with additional raisins and walnuts. Seal tightly. Attach instructions.

Instructions:

Empty cookie mix into a medium bowl. Stir in 1/2 cup softened butter, one beaten egg and one teaspoon vanilla extract; mix well. Shape into one-inch balls; arrange on greased baking sheets. Bake at 375 degrees for 10 to 12 minutes or until cookies are golden. Makes 2-1/2 dozen.

There are no bells in
all the world so sweet
as sleigh bells over snow.
-Elizabeth Coatsworth

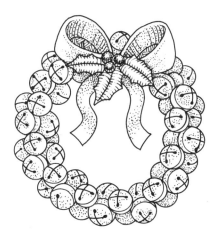

Cranberry-Pecan Cookie Mix in a Jar

Kay Marone
Des Moines, IA

Instead of cranberries, we've tried raisins in this mix too...
just as delicious.

2/3 c. sweetened, dried
   cranberries
1/2 c. chopped pecans
1/2 c. dark brown sugar, packed

2 c. buttermilk biscuit
   baking mix, divided
1/2 c. light brown sugar, packed

Layer cranberries, pecans, dark brown sugar, one cup biscuit baking
mix, light brown sugar and remaining baking mix in a one-quart,
wide-mouth canning jar, pressing after each layer to pack. Fill any
additional space at the top of the jar with additional cranberries and
pecans. Seal tightly. Attach instructions.

Instructions:

Empty cookie mix into a medium bowl. Stir in 1/2 cup softened butter,
one beaten egg and one teaspoon vanilla extract; mix well. Shape into
one-inch balls; arrange on greased baking sheets. Bake at 375 degrees
for 10 to 12 minutes or until cookies are golden. Makes 2-1/2 dozen.

String fresh cranberries onto wire and shape into a
heart, star or initial for a pretty jar tie-on.

206

Hot Orange-Spice Drink Mix

Tina Wright
Atlanta, GA

It will warm you head to toe...great for after sledding!

10-oz. jar orange drink mix
1/4 c. lemonade mix
2 c. powdered sugar

2 t. cinnamon
1 t. ground cloves

Combine all ingredients together; mix well. Pour into a one-quart, wide-mouth canning jar and pack firmly. Seal tightly and decorate as desired. Attach instructions. Makes about 3-1/2 cups.

Pour 2-1/2 teaspoons drink mix into a mug. Add one cup boiling water. Stir to dissolve. Makes one serving.

Hazelnut Cookie Mix in a Jar

Cheri Maxwell
Gulf Breeze, FL

If you can't find hazelnuts, use walnuts, pecans or macadamias.
Although the taste will be slightly different, this cookie mix will
still make the most delicious, crunchy cookies.

1 c. hazelnuts, chopped
   and toasted
1/2 c. dark brown sugar, packed

2 c. buttermilk biscuit
   baking mix
1/2 c. light brown sugar, packed

Layer hazelnuts, dark brown sugar, one cup biscuit baking mix, light brown sugar and remaining baking mix in a one-quart, wide-mouth canning jar, pressing after each layer to pack. Fill any additional space at the top of the jar with additional hazelnuts. Seal tightly. Attach instructions.

Instructions:

Empty cookie mix into a medium bowl. Stir in 1/2 cup softened butter, one beaten egg and one teaspoon vanilla extract; mix well. Shape into one-inch balls; arrange on greased baking sheets. Bake at 375 degrees for 10 to 12 minutes or until cookies are golden. Makes 2-1/2 dozen.

Whoever is happy will make others happy too.
—Anne Frank

Merry Mocha Cappuccino Mix

Geneva Rogers
Gillette, WY

I've packaged this mix in decorative glass bottles with corks and vintage blue glass canning jars with zinc lids. Keep an eye open at sales for unique containers.

1-1/4 c. powdered
   non-dairy creamer
6 T. plus 2 t. instant espresso
   coffee powder

1/2 c. plus 2 T. powdered sugar
3 T. plus 1 t. baking cocoa
2 t. cinnamon

Combine all ingredients; mix well and pour into an airtight container, pressing to pack. Seal tightly. Attach instructions. Makes about 2-1/2 cups.

Instructions:

Pour 4 tablespoons drink mix into a mug. Add one cup boiling water and stir to dissolve. Makes one serving.

Have a breakfast get-together for friends
& neighbors. Serve pancakes, juices and fruit,
then send everyone home with jars of
Merry Mocha Cappuccino Mix...how neighborly!

Double-Fudge Brownie Mix in a Jar

Kelly Alderson
Erie, PA

I like to use a funnel to layer all the ingredients into jars...less mess!

2 c. sugar
1 c. baking cocoa
1 c. all-purpose flour

1 c. chopped pecans
1 c. semi-sweet chocolate chips

Layer all ingredients in the order given, pressing after each layer to pack, in a one-quart, wide-mouth canning jar. Seal tightly. Attach instructions.

Instructions:

Cream one cup softened butter in a large bowl with an electric mixer on high setting; add 4 eggs, beating well after each addition. Add brownie mix and beat until smooth. Spread into a greased and floured 13"x9" baking pan. Bake at 325 degrees for 40 to 50 minutes, until a toothpick inserted into the center comes out clean. Cut into bars. Makes 1-1/2 dozen.

Use decorative-edge scissors to spruce up old holiday greeting cards... easy gift tags!

Gammy's Best Hot Chocolate Mix

Linda Fleisher
Akron, OH

*My family loves hot chocolate and this is the best we've ever tasted!
This recipe makes a lot, so you may want to divide the recipe in half.
But then again, it's nice to have a whole winter's supply!*

4-lb. pkg. powdered milk
2 15-oz. pkgs. chocolate
   drink mix
2 16-oz. pkgs. powdered sugar
16-oz. jar powdered
   non-dairy creamer

2 3.9-oz. pkgs. instant
   chocolate pudding mix
10-1/2 oz. pkg. mini
   marshmallows

Combine all ingredients; mix well. Pour into three, one-gallon airtight
containers. Seal tightly and attach instructions. Makes about 3 gallons.

Instructions:

Pour about 1/3 cup mix into a mug; add one cup boiling water.
Stir to dissolve. Makes one serving.

*Pair a cocoa mix with some new cozy slippers or flannel
pajamas...sure to be welcome on frosty mornings.*

Gingerbread Creamer Mix

Kimberly Pfleiderer
Galion, OH

Spoon this creamer mix into a syrup pourer, then tie on the instructions with a length of raffia. The syrup pourer makes adding this mix to cups of coffee or tea so simple!

2 c. powdered non-dairy creamer
1/2 c. brown sugar, packed
1 t. cinnamon
1/2 t. allspice
1/2 t. ground cloves
1/4 t. ground ginger
1/4 t. nutmeg

Combine all ingredients in an airtight container; mix well. Seal tightly and attach instructions. Makes about 2-3/4 cups.

Instructions:

Pour one heaping teaspoonful of mix in a mug of hot coffee or tea. Stir to dissolve. Makes one serving.

Fill a pretty sugar bowl with Gingerbread Creamer Mix and tie on a dainty silver spoon...a thoughtful gift for any occasion.

Coconut-Raisin Cookie Mix in a Jar

Megan Brooks
Antioch, TN

Always a welcome gift for busy elves!

1/2 c. sugar
1/2 c. raisins
1-1/4 c. flaked coconut
1 c. corn flake cereal, crushed
3/4 c. brown sugar, packed

1/2 c. quick-cooking oats,
  uncooked
1-1/4 c. all-purpose flour
1 t. baking soda
1 t. baking powder

Layer sugar, raisins, coconut, cereal, brown sugar and oats in a one-quart, wide-mouth canning jar, pressing to pack after each layer. Set aside. Combine flour, baking soda and baking powder in a bowl; add to jar. Press to pack and seal jar tightly. Attach instructions.

Instructions:

Empty cookie mix into a large bowl; mix to combine. Stir in 1/2 cup softened butter, one egg and one teaspoon vanilla extract. Mix until completely blended. Roll dough into walnut-size balls and arrange 2 inches apart on greased baking sheets. Bake at 350 degrees for 8 to 10 minutes until golden. Let cool on baking sheets for 5 minutes; remove to wire racks to cool completely. Makes 2-1/2 dozen.

Stencil a snowflake design on the outside of a jar mix or slip a tiny evergreen wreath around the jar neck...don't forget the bow.

Blonde Brownie Mix in a Jar

Sharon Tillman
Hampton, VA

A new twist on an old favorite, these brownies are made with coconut, but no chocolate. So tasty, you may want to bake a batch for yourself.

1/2 c. flaked coconut
1/2 c. sugar
2 c. brown sugar, packed

2 c. all-purpose flour
1-1/2 t. baking powder
1/4 t. salt

Layer coconut, sugar and brown sugar in a one-quart, wide-mouth canning jar, pressing after each layer to pack. Set aside. Combine flour, baking powder and salt; mix well and add to jar. Press firmly; seal jar tightly. Attach instructions.

Instructions:

Empty brownie mix into a large mixing bowl; mix well. Add 3/4 cup softened butter, 2 beaten eggs and 2 teaspoons vanilla extract. Mix until completely blended; spread into a greased 13"x9" baking pan. Bake at 375 degrees for 25 minutes; let cool and cut into squares. Makes 2 dozen.

Set the mood at a holiday cookie exchange with jolly Christmas music! Ask friends to bring along their own favorite music to share too.

Hot Malted Cocoa Mix

John Alexander
New Britain, CT

I like to give jars of cocoa mix with cookie kits. I just fill a pail with cookie dough, icing and all the extras to finish the cookies. Moms love it and the kids do too!

25-1/2 oz. pkg. powdered milk
6 c. miniature marshmallows
16-oz. pkg. instant chocolate
   milk mix
13-oz. jar malted milk powder

1 c. powdered sugar
6-oz. jar powdered
   non-dairy creamer
1/2 t. salt

Combine all ingredients in a large bowl; mix well. Divide evenly into five, one-quart, wide-mouth canning jars. Seal tightly. Attach instructions. Makes 5 jars.

Instructions:

Pour 1/3 cup mix into a mug; add 3/4 cup boiling water and stir to dissolve. Makes one serving.

Invitations can be edible too! Cut gingerbread into postcard sizes and bake. When cool, pipe on royal icing with all the party details...yummy!

Chocolate-Raisin Cookie Mix in a Jar

Diana Chaney
Olathe, KS

Sometimes we swap out the chocolate for vanilla yogurt raisins.

3/4 c. sugar
1/2 c. brown sugar, packed
1 c. chocolate-covered raisins
1/2 c. milk chocolate chips

1-3/4 c. all-purpose flour
1 t. baking powder
1/2 t. baking soda

Layer sugar, brown sugar, raisins and chocolate chips in a one-quart, wide-mouth canning jar, pressing after each layer to pack. Set aside. Blend flour, baking powder and baking soda; add to jar and press to pack. Seal tightly. Attach instructions.

Instructions:

Empty cookie mix into a large mixing bowl. Add 1/2 cup softened butter, one beaten egg and one teaspoon vanilla extract. Mix well; shape into walnut-size balls. Arrange 2 inches apart on baking sheets lined with parchment paper. Bake at 375 degrees for 13 to 15 minutes until golden. Cool 5 minutes on baking sheets; remove to wire racks and cool completely. Makes 2-1/2 dozen.

Don't forget your letter carrier...slip a tin of goodies or a jar mix into your mailbox for a special surprise.

French Vanilla Cocoa Mix

Robin Hill
Rochester, NY

I really like the sweet, creamy taste of this cocoa mix.

10-1/2 c. powdered milk
4 c. powdered sugar
2 8-oz. jars French vanilla-
    flavored powdered
    non-dairy creamer

3-1/2 c. hot chocolate mix
2-3/4 c. powdered
    non-dairy creamer
1/2 t. salt

Combine all ingredients in a large bowl; mix well. Divide evenly into eight, one-quart wide-mouth canning jars. Seal tightly. Attach instructions. Makes 8 jars.

Instructions:

Pour 3 heaping tablespoonfuls mix into a mug; add boiling water or hot milk. Stir to dissolve. Makes one serving.

Set jar mixes inside a child's wagon or on a sled placed by the front door...guests can take a yummy mix home as a party favor.

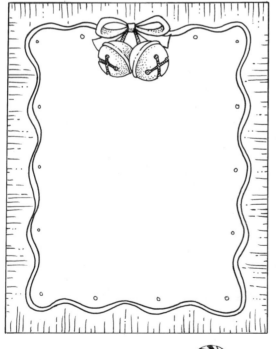

1. Copy
2. Color
3. Cut out
4. Share

To:

From:

To:

From:

Index

Index

Index

Send us your favorite recipe!

and the memory that makes it special for you!* If we select your recipe for a brand-new **Gooseberry Patch** cookbook, your name will appear right along with it...and you'll receive a FREE copy of the book.

Share your recipe on our website at
www.gooseberrypatch.com

Or mail to:
Gooseberry Patch • Attn: Cookbook Dept.
2500 Farmers Drive, Suite 110
Columbus, OH 43235

*Don't forget to include your name, address, phone number and email address so we'll know how to reach you for your FREE book!

Find Gooseberry Patch
wherever you are!

www.gooseberrypatch.com

Call us toll-free at 1•800•854•6673

U.S. to Metric Recipe Equivalents

Volume Measurements

1/4 teaspoon	1 mL
1/2 teaspoon	2 mL
1 teaspoon	5 mL
1 tablespoon = 3 teaspoons	15 mL
2 tablespoons = 1 fluid ounce	30 mL
1/4 cup	60 mL
1/3 cup	75 mL
1/2 cup = 4 fluid ounces	125 mL
1 cup = 8 fluid ounces	250 mL
2 cups = 1 pint =16 fluid ounces	500 mL
4 cups = 1 quart	1 L

Weights

1 ounce	30 g
4 ounces	120 g
8 ounces	225 g
16 ounces = 1 pound	450 g

Oven Temperatures

300° F	150° C
325° F	160° C
350° F	180° C
375° F	190° C
400° F	200° C
450° F	230° C

Baking Pan Sizes

Square

8x8x2 inches	2 L = 20x20x5 cm
9x9x2 inches	2.5 L = 23x23x5 cm

Rectangular

13x9x2 inches	3.5 L = 33x23x5 cm

Loaf

9x5x3 inches	2 L = 23x13x7 cm

Round

8x1-1/2 inches	1.2 L = 20x4 cm
9x1-1/2 inches	1.5 L = 23x4 cm